In the
Fullness
of Time

In the
Fullness
of Time

Christ-Centered Wisdom
for the Third Millennium

FULTON J. SHEEN

Compiled and Edited
by Patricia A. Kossmann

LIGUORI/TRIUMPH
LIGUORI, MISSOURI

Published by Liguori/Triumph
An Imprint of Liguori Publications
Liguori, Missouri
http://www.liguori.org

Library of Congress Cataloging-in-Publication Data

Sheen, Fulton J. (Fulton John), 1895–1979.
    In the fullness of time : Christ-centered wisdom for the third millennium / Fulton J. Sheen ; compiled and edited by Patricia A. Kossmann. — 1st ed.
       p.   cm.
    ISBN 0-7648-0509-6 (pb)
    1. Christian life—Catholic authors. I. Kossmann, Patricia A. II. Title.
    BX2350.2.S455   1999
    248.4'82—dc21   99–23335

Printed in the United States of America
03 02 01 00 99   5 4 3 2 1
First Edition

We are challenged to participate in the sufferings of God in the hands of a godless world, without attempting to gloss over the ungodliness with a veneer of religion or trying to transfigure it. It is not a religious act which makes a Christian what he is, but participation in the suffering of God in the life of the world.

Dietrich Bonhoeffer,
Letters and Papers from Prison

Contents

Contents

Foreword

THIS COMPENDIUM IS offered in commemoration of the twentieth anniversary of the death of Archbishop Fulton J. Sheen in 1979. But, of course, the contents are as timeless as Truth and Life itself. As the world awaits the third millennium—in some cases with expectant joy and hope, in others perhaps with stark trepidation—we pray, we dialogue, we wonder...we believe.

We believe in the good Lord's care and providence. We believe in his love. We believe in his presence among us. Indeed, as Christians we believe he is with us now, with us until the end of time. "His words of heavenly wisdom were not allowed to fade away on an evening breeze," Sheen reminds us, "but were caught up by his four evangelists." So we believe he is the *fullness* of life, the *fullness* of time. And more, we who believe are called to live in that fullness each and every day. As Archbishop Sheen puts it, the distance of centuries cannot separate us from Christ, who lives on in his words, his teaching, his example.

> [O]ur Lord can influence our day because he has left us a beautiful example of a holy, moral life that we should follow. We, too, can be forgiving, as he forgave those who crucified him; we can be gentle, as he was gentle to little children; humble as he was before those who would make him an earthly king, and prayerful as he was in the long vigils on the mountaintops. Countless, indeed, are the heroic, self-sacrificing, and saintly deeds of our own day, which have had as their inspiration the example of him who left the heavens to teach

us to be the kind of people God from all eternity wished us to be.

It is Ash Wednesday as I put these thoughts on paper. A day—indeed, the first day of many—for "going to my room," going within, and looking at who and what I am in relation to my God and my salvation. With eyes focused on the Cross, in the presence of him who is my liberator, my savior, I am once again grateful to Bishop Sheen for all that he has written and preached about the Cross. There's no denying the centrality of the Cross to the Christian faith. As Sheen often expressed it, "Without the Cross there would be no crown"; or "Without Good Friday there would be no Easter Sunday." We are connected, one and all, to that Cross; and through that Cross to one another. Connected in hope and joy.

The contents of this book, drawn primarily from some of Sheen's radio talks and retreat conferences, point clearly and sharply to that connection: the oneness of all in the Body of Christ, who is both our center and our foundation. No matter what the topic, we see in these pages how everything springs from, and falls back to, Christ. Various essays explore such topics as sacrifice, solidarity, prayer, emptying and filling, Mary's vital role as Mother of the Church, the soul of the Church, reparation, liberation, service, and sanctification. Throughout these pages we are challenged, perhaps even chastened, but continually uplifted, enspirited, and strengthened in our Christian faith. Above all, our focus is brought gently and quietly back to the centrality of the God-man Christ, without whom we simply flail about, as a small boat in a raging sea.

Amidst all the hoopla about the approaching new millennium, all the gloom- and doomsayers, it would be good to read and reflect upon the words in this book. They are for *now* and the coming age. They speak truth for all time, although it's sometimes difficult to hear that truth. They invite and encourage us to *go within, go to our room,* contemplate our life, and listen for the Word—and not only during Lent, but in every season of the year. One of the pieces in this book is entitled "First Come, Then Go." It sums up, I think, the core of our Christian obligation: *Come and see where I live.* Then: *Go into the world.* The message here, as throughout, gives us much to hang onto and rejoice about, not unlike a welcome rescue from that raging sea mentioned above.

And so we greet the new year, the new century, the two-thousandth year since the Lord's coming among us—coming as one of us—with renewed faith and purpose. Just as Fulton Sheen greeted every new day, every new encounter with the living Christ in the Blessed Sacrament, every new opportunity to bring Christ and his message to people across the lands. What a beautiful example he has given us. In fact, a challenge: to *be* Christ in the world!

This book, then, is cause for celebration: celebration of our life, our faith, our destiny, our God. It is my hope that we take its words to heart, think about them, break them as bread, and share them with others. They can be plentiful food for the journey that still lies before us, for they speak of a fullness that we can only imagine while on earth. We are grateful for Fulton Sheen's wisdom, counsel, inspiration, and living faith. No doubt he claimed his heavenly reward twenty years ago. As the world now stands poised to greet the third millennium, would that people everywhere come to recognize and celebrate the oneness of the global family. Would that people come to see the hand of a loving God stretched out equally over all. Would that the meaning and message of the Cross permeate the world.

And may all of us always rejoice in the Cause of our salvation. God love you!

Patricia A. Kossmann
Literary Representative
THE ESTATE OF FULTON J. SHEEN

One

Life Begins at Birth

NEVER HAS THERE BEEN a greater untruth, and never will there be, than "life begins at forty." That phrase is merely the aged's justification for growing old against their will, a soothing ointment for lost vigor and faded beauty which can never be strong and fresh again. I can understand why a hoary old world should put a premium on age, for the world wants the sympathy of those who grow old with her; but I cannot understand why anyone whose vision is broader than the years and whose hopes are higher than an ivy vine should value age above youth. Anyone with the vaguest understanding of either the world of nature or the world of grace knows that life does not begin at forty. Life begins at birth.

There are other introductions to life than the opening of the womb, either the womb of the great portals of flesh or the womb of the baptismal font—the one begetting us as children of humans, the other as children of God. Religion, by its very nature, has something to do with birth and, therefore, with youth. Doesn't all religious history reveal that the closer we get to God the younger we become and, therefore, the more like children? Thus, it might well be that as we grow old in years we grow young in God. But how can we grow younger as we grow older?

Answer me this question: What is youthfulness? Youthfulness is proximity to the source of life. A child of four is younger than a child of six because he is two years closer to

1

the source of life: his parents. A person of twenty is younger than a person of forty because he is twenty years closer to the source of life: his parents.

Now, we have another source of life besides our parents, namely, God. Hence, the closer we get to God the younger we become. And so true is this, that the day on which saints *die* the Church calls *natalitia*. The world celebrates a birthday on the day we are born to temporal life; the Church celebrates a birthday on the day on which we are born to eternal life. But in either case: Life begins at birth.

The other side of the picture is this: Not only do we become younger and more like children the nearer we get to God, but the closer God gets to us the more he becomes a child. God never came so close to us as in the Incarnation, and then he appeared as a *babe*. The reason Christmas is the happiest day of the year is because it is a birthday—not the fortieth, but the first! God might have revealed himself to us in all the full bloom and blossom of a triumphant king of twoscore years; he might have canonized maturity by making his life begin at forty—but he actually began it as a child. And to the eternal confusion of those who value age above youth he completed his life work, finished his Father's business, while still in his early thirties. Who, then, will say that life begins at forty?

There is no escape from the tremendous fact of Christmas day, that when God revealed himself to this poor world of ours, men cried in astonishment: "Why, it is a child!" And so it is that the closer we get to God the more we become children, and the closer God gets to us the more he becomes a child. No one in the world ever suspected that the Ancient of Days who presided at creation would take his throne in that creation as a babe in a crib, just as no one ever thought he would tell the old men of forty, like Nicodemus, that they must be born again. According to all worldly standards, it is the aged who are learned. And yet when Wisdom came to earth he was a child, and when Wise Men came to Wisdom they were told to be like children. Christmas, then, is the coronation of childhood, the glorification of the young whose hearts are simple, the proclamation to aging hearts that the world need not despair and die, because the Fountain of Youth has come into it with his quickening drafts, to unburden the years, turn time backward, make old things young again.

Christmas, then, is the solemn day when God becomes a child, when we become children, and where we all meet at a crib. The aging old world is already jaded with its memory, for it believes that life begins at forty. But we who will see Bethlehem again every Christmas morn, and receive the babe not in our arms but in our hearts, know the world is wrong. Life begins at birth!

Two

Love Prayer

IT IS OBJECTED THAT there is much repetition in the Rosary because the Lord's Prayer and the Hail Mary are said so often; therefore it is monotonous. That reminds me of a woman who came to see me one evening after instructions. She said, "I would never become a Catholic. You say the same words in the Rosary over and over again, and anyone who repeats the same words is never sincere. I would never believe anyone who repeated his words, and neither would God." I asked her who the man with her was. She said he was her fiancé. I asked, "Does he love you?" "Certainly he does." "But how do you know?" "He told me." "What did he say?" "He said, 'I love you.'" "When did he tell you last?" "About an hour ago." "Did he tell you before?" "Yes, last night." "What did he say?" "'I love you.'" "But never before?" "He tells me every night."

Then I told her, "Do not believe him. He is repeating; he is not sincere."

The beautiful truth is that there is *no* repetition in "I love you." Because they are spoken in a new moment of time, another point in space, the words do not mean the same as they did at another time or in another space. A mother says to her son, "You are a good boy." She may have said it ten thousand times before, but each time it means something different. The whole personality goes out to it anew, as a new historical circumstance summons forth a new outburst of affection. Love is never monotonous in the uniformity of its expression. The mind is infinitely variable in its language, but the heart is not. The heart of a man, in the face of the woman he loves, is too poor to translate the infinity of his affection into a different word. So the heart takes one expression, "I love you," and in saying it over and over again, never repeats itself.

That is what we do when we say the Rosary. We are saying to God, to the Trinity, to the Incarnate Savior, to the Blessed Mother, "I love you, I love you, I love you." Each time it means something different because, at each decade, our mind is moving to a new demonstration of the Savior's love: for example, from the mystery of his love which willed to become one of us in his Incarnation, to the other mystery of love when he suffered for us, and on to the other mystery of his love where he intercedes for us before the heavenly Father. And who shall forget that our Lord himself, in the moment of his greatest agony, repeated, three times within an hour, the same prayer?

We often speak to people while our minds are thinking of something else. But in the Rosary, we not only *say* the prayers, we *think* them. Bethlehem, Galilee, Nazareth, Jerusalem, Golgotha, Calvary, Mount Olivet, heaven: All these move before our mind's eye as we pray. The stained-glass windows in a church invite the eye to dwell on thoughts about God. The Rosary invites our fingers, our lips, and our heart in one vast symphony of prayer, and for that reason it is the greatest prayer ever composed.

The Rosary is the best therapy for distraught, unhappy, fearful, and frustrated souls, precisely because it involves the simultaneous use of three powers: the physical, the vocal, and the spiritual—in that order. The fingers, touching the beads, are reminded that these little counters are to be used for prayer. This is the *physical* suggestion of prayer.

The lips move in unison with the fingers. This is the second, the *vocal*, suggestion of prayer. The Church, a wise psychologist, insists that the lips move while saying the Rosary because she knows that the external rhythm of the body can create a rhythm of the soul. If the fingers and the lips keep at it, the *spiritual* will soon follow, and the prayer will eventually end in the heart.

The physical and the mental work together if we give them a chance. Stronger minds can work from the mind outward; but worried minds have to work from the outside inward. However, in being faithful to the Rosary, little by little, you will be surprised how you can climb out of your worries and fears, bead by bead, up to the very throne of the Heart of Love itself.

Three

Complicity

Feel a self-reproachful complicity
In every crime on page one.
Feel every man's sin as your own
As a mother feels a daughter's pains.
Take another's sickness unto your own
As "He bore our infirmities."

Against a wall with arms outstretched
A wife in sobbing tears didst fling herself
At the husband's tale of another woman
And he at the sight of it did say:
"At that moment I saw Christ hanging
    on the Cross."
The lesser cross revealed the greater Cross,
In which Love is wounded by our sins.

Only the wounded know how to bind up wounds:
The converted sinner has more mercy than
    the sinless Pharisee;
True helpers are those who have been
    bombed out.
Hence He, in the words of Scripture,
"Has compassion on our infirmities."

You are not alone! You are on a team!

Hurt, they carry you to the sidelines.
"Why should this happen to me?" you ask—
Forgetful that you helped the team to win.
No suffering is wasted!
As clouds carry rain over mountains,
So your patience with cancer,
Your resignation to withered limbs
Redounds to some soul in Ceylon,
And helps a missionary in Seoul.

The greatest tragedy is not what people suffer
But that they have no one whom they love
To whom they can offer their cross.
This is wasted pain—
The pain of the cross, not the Crucifix;
The guillotine, not the oneness with Christ.

Four

The Whole Christ

HOW DOES JESUS OF NAZARETH INFLUENCE me who am centuries removed from him by time and thousands of miles by space? The answer is that there are several ways in which any person may influence posterity, even long after his or her death. And the first of these is by teaching. Anyone who ever wrote or spoke profound truths may echo himself from the grave.

Thanks to their teaching, the wisdom of the Greeks lives among us. Plato and Aristotle are enshrined in our universities, and professors talk of them as if they had walked with them through the marketplaces and porches of Athens. Augustine of the fifth century and Aquinas of the thirteenth are made to come from their graves, and by their written word instruct our hearts, minds, and souls in the things of God and humanity. And who is there who will deny that George Washington and Abraham Lincoln live beyond their day by their state papers, so full of the finest political traditions of a free people?

Our Blessed Lord can influence us in precisely the same way. His words of heavenly wisdom were not allowed to fade away on an evening breeze, but were caught up by his four evangelists—Matthew, Mark, Luke, and John—so that all who could read or hear would know the wisdom of One who spoke, not as the scribes and Pharisees, but as one having authority, even the authority of God. The Scriptures, then, constitute the first great link between the past and the present, between his earthly life and our modern existence.

But there is a second way in which characters of the past may make themselves felt in the present, and that is by example. Anyone who has had a biographer or who has written the incidents of his own life, may project the force of his personality into the future long after his flesh has crumbled into a heap of molded dust. The military example of a Caesar or a Napoleon, the saintly life of a Vincent de Paul or a Don Bosco, the daring exploits of a Columbus or a Magellan, can be told and retold a thousand times, and thus become an inspiration and a challenge to saintly and brave individuals of other times and different climes.

In like manner our Lord can influence our day because he has left us a beautiful example of a holy, moral life that we should follow. We, too, can be forgiving as he forgave those who crucified him; we can be gentle as he was gentle to little children, humble as he was before those who would make him an earthly king, and prayerful as he was in the long vigils on the mountaintops. Countless, indeed, are the heroic, self-sacrificing, and saintly deeds of our own day, which have had as their inspiration the example of him who left the heavens to teach us to be the kind of people God from all eternity wished us to be.

If our Lord had no other way to energize hearts and minds than the two ways common to all, then Christianity is only the memory of a man who lived and died; it is no more worth preserving than any human religion. Modern milk-and-water Christianity regards the life of Christ as nothing more than the life of a good man, and because it bids us look back [two thousand] years to Israel and Judea, because it merely repeats his words, reinterprets his actions, and recalls his example, as it might do that of Scipio or Aurelius, it has lost its hold on the modern soul. If that were all Christianity were, then it should die, for people cannot be influenced long by a mere memory, however noble; it is the curse of a sin-stricken humanity quickly to forget even the finest heritages of the past.

Christianity, fortunately, is something more than a memory, because our Lord is something more than a man. He is true God and true man. Being God he can perpetuate himself not only by his teaching and his example, which are means common to everyone, but also in a third way, which belongs to him alone as God: by his life. Others may leave their titles, their wealth, their stocks and their bonds, their doctrines and their biographies, but only our Lord can make a last will and testament bequeathing to posterity that which no one else on dying could ever leave: his life and the life of the world.

There are really three phases to the complete life of Christ: His earthly life, his glorified life, and his mystical life. Without any one of them we know not Christ. Those who consider only the earthly life of Christ either develop a sentimental spirituality or end up regarding him only as a good man and a teacher of humanitarian ethics. Those who consider him only in his heavenly life of glory regard him as an absentee landlord disregarding both his promise to send his Spirit and his abiding interest in the souls he came to save.

So the whole Christ embraces not only the earthly life in which he redeemed, but also the glorified and mystical life by which he pours out the fruits of redemption upon the world. For the present it suffices us to know that he is not only our Truth because of his teaching, not only our Way because of his example, but also our Life because he is our Savior and Redeemer.

His life is not something gone from us, but living among us, making our lives livable, hopeful, and glad. Our eyes need not look back to Bethlehem, for the Wise Men and the simple shepherds are still at the feet of Christ. There is nothing past in him who is eternal. There are no memories of him who is the "same yesterday, today, and tomorrow." There are no distances from here to Galilee, for he who is divine has pitched his tent in the very center of our hearts and civilization—because he is Eternal Life.

Five

The Soul of the Church

THE CHURCH IS THE BODY of Christ, composed of the many millions of individuals who have been incorporated to it by baptism, and governed by the invisible head, Christ, and the visible head, the Vicar of Christ on earth. But a body and a head are not sufficient to constitute the Mystical Christ as the Church. The Church must also have a soul as the principle of its life and its unity. That soul is the Holy Spirit.

In order that we may properly understand the role of the Holy Spirit, the third person of the Blessed Trinity, try to picture the apostles and the faithful on earth during the ten days after the Ascension of our Lord into heaven. The Church then existed in its raw material—its great arteries had been formed, its head had been named, its members were called, but it still lacked a soul.

The condition of the Church at this time may be imperfectly likened to America before the drawing up of the Declaration of Independence. The Dutch, the English, the French, the Irish, the Scotch, and the other nationalities were scattered up and down the Atlantic seaboard, but there was no common bond or spirit holding them together. They needed unity—a soul to make them one. That spark came in the Declaration of Independence, which fired them with the spirit of free-born American people. The Church was somewhat in this position. The apostles and disciples and the faithful were still separate individuals; they needed a soul to make

15

them one. But here the analogy breaks down. The spirit which was to make the members of the Church one was different from the spirit that made America one.

The condition of the Church can be represented better by the analogy of life. Its members were like the elements in a chemical laboratory, capable of being part of a body, and yet not a body because lacking a soul. We know up to one hundred percent the chemicals that enter into the constitution of a human body, and yet with all our superior knowledge of chemistry, we cannot make a body in our laboratories. Why? Because we lack the power to give a unifying principle, a soul, to those chemicals which will make them mutually coalesce into that new emergent we call life.

Now the apostles were like the chemicals in a laboratory; they were individuals, each with his own outlook on life, each with his doubts, his uncertainties, his points of view. They could not give themselves unity any more than chemicals alone can make life. The permanent union of their minds was impossible without a certitude from on high, for life is not a push from below, but a gift from above. They needed a soul, a spirit—a vivifying, unifying principle which would make the cells of the Mystical Body cohere in the unity of a headship under Christ. And this vivifying, unifying spirit did not come until the day of Pentecost.

The apostles knew the Spirit would come to them. They would never forget the beautiful way in which our Lord promised his spirit the night before he died:

> I have yet many things to say to you: but you cannot bear them now. But when he, the Spirit of truth, is come, he will teach you all truth.... And I will ask the Father, and he shall give you another Paraclete, that he may abide with you forever.

This was only a promise of the Spirit that was to come. But our Lord keeps his promises. Accordingly, ten days after the Ascension, the apostles with Peter as their head were in solitude in the Cenacle where the Savior had instituted the Eucharist and appeared to doubting Thomas.

And suddenly there came a sound from heaven, as of a mighty wind coming, and it filled the whole house where they were sitting. And there appeared to them parted tongues as it were of fire, and it sat upon every one of them: and they were all filled with the Holy Spirit (Acts 2:2–4).

In the fiery glow of that Pentecostal gift the individuals, the cells of the Mystical Body, like the bones in the vision of Ezekiel, were drawn together into a living body, animated by the Eternal Spirit of the Third Person of the Blessed Trinity. The scattered rays now emerged into the light of the world. All they had dimly guessed at and faintly perceived now became absolute certainty in the glow of the Pentecostal fire, as they saw the continuity of Nazareth and the Cenacle: For as Christ had taken his physical body from the womb of the Virgin Mary overshadowed by the Holy Spirit, so now was Christ taking from the womb of humanity his Mystical Body overshadowed by the Pentecostal Spirit. The Church was now created in the strictest sense of the term— it had its head, Christ; its soul, the Holy Spirit; and us, its body.

Organization has nothing to do with the marvelous vitality of the Church, nor is there any other human explanation. If the Church were left to its human elements it would have perished long ago. The secret of her immortal life is her Eternal Spirit, which cannot be destroyed by the world any more than the soul of an infant can be destroyed. Hence in the face of the force of violence the Spirit manifests the immortality of her being; against the force of ideas the Spirit shows the immortality of her ideas; and against the force of passion the Spirit shows the immortality of her love.

If there is any picture that adequately describes the Church in time, it is that of a person living throughout the cataclysms and revolutions, the progress and the unfolding of the centuries. A person who is fifty today is the same identical person as always, despite the changes in his bodily life and the historical upheavals of our time. He can say, "I saw mankind exalt itself to a god in the pre-war period; I saw that same humanity prove it was not a god but only a beast in the battlefields of the World War[s]; I saw it settle down to a false peace without ever learning the lesson that it cannot survive without God." In like manner, the Church is an abiding Person through all centuries. The only difference between her now and then is the difference between the acorn and the oak, the mustard seed and the great tree. Her members have come and gone, like the cells in a human body, but her Spirit has remained one and the same.

And since it is the Spirit that makes the Body, the Church which is the Mystical Body of Christ has been contemporaneous with the centuries. When, therefore, we in the twentieth century wish to know about Christ, about his early Church, about history, we go not only to the dusty records but to the living Church:

> I have adapted myself to every form of government the world has ever known; I have lived with Caesars and kings, tyrants and dictators, parliaments and presidents, monarchies and republics. I have welcomed every advance of science, and were it not for me the great records of the pagan world would not have been preserved. It is true I have not changed my doctrine, but that is because "the doctrine is not

mine but his that sent me." I change my garments, which belong to time, but not my Spirit, which belongs to eternity. In the course of my long life, I have seen so many modern ideas become unmodern, that I know I shall live to chant a requiem over the modern ideas of this day as I chanted it over the modern ideas of the last century.

I shall grow weak when my members become rich and cease to pray, but I shall never die. I shall be crucified as I was on Calvary, but I shall rise again, and finally when time shall be no more, and I shall have grown to my full stature, then shall I be taken into heaven as the bride of my Head, Christ.

Six

The Victim of Love

You think you swept all love away
As many autumns shook the years like leaves.
'Til now all your loves
Were as a barter and exchange:
The sweet reciprocal: "I love you; you love Me."

But two deeper loves are left you still:
One to be used in time;
The other, in eternity.

The first, the seeming unreciprocated love
Wherein you love Him Who left a wound,
Though He in turn is silent.
But you, like Job, cry out:
"I will love Him though He slay me."

To love Him because we *feel* His love
Is to be repaid a thousandfold.
But to love through a dumb and un-echoing love
Is to be one with Him
Who in the body-shuddering solitude of the Cross
Felt so unloved by man.

This arm-less, lip-less love
Which seems so cold
Is but the novitiate to that other Love
Which awaits thee in eternity
Wherein you shall be dumb and speechless
With ecstasies of *Jesu, voluptas cordium.*

Seven

Infallible Truth

CHRIST'S COMING INTO THE WORLD was not like that of a sight-seer to a strange city, but rather like that of an artist visiting his own studio, or an author paging the books he himself has written, for in becoming incarnate the Divine Word was tabernacling himself in his own creation. His human nature in no way limited his Divine Wisdom, but it did give him a new way of communicating it to humans, and one quite comfortable to their own nature. Through a human tongue like their own, speaking their own dialect, people heard him say, "I am the light of the world"; they saw his lips move, and for the first time in the history of the world they heard one equate himself with Truth, saying to Pilate, "I am come to give testimony to the truth."

Now it is quite unthinkable that all this Wisdom should be lost, for it is the Truth of God himself. It is even unthinkable that he who was so emphatic about every "iota" of his Truth being accepted, and who condemned those who would not believe, and who remained three years on earth to teach its details to the tardy intellects of his time, and who died rather than surrender the Truth of what he taught, should allow this same Divine Truth to be forgotten, to be twisted, turned, misinterpreted, interpolated, and explained away as if it were worth no more than the babble of a child.

One need only recall how the earthly wisdom of an Aristotle was altered by his disciples to realize the need of an agency to preserve truth. It hardly seems consonant with the nature of God to allow the branches of his Vine to be poisoned, or to go back on his promise that he would send the Spirit of Truth which would preserve his followers from the specter of evil and the gates of hell.

If God in the providential ordering of the universe bestows on vegetables and plants and flowers the power of drawing up from the soil and out of the atmosphere what is good for them, and rejecting what is evil; if he has implanted in the birds and beasts an unerring instinct which enables them to ward off the forces of decay and preserve the original endowment of life; if he gives to man the light of reason to enable him to choose what is good for his human perfection and reject that which cannot be healthfully incorporated into his moral fiber; if God has answered the cry of hunger on the lips of a newborn babe with the chalice of nourishment in the heart of a mother; if he has met the cry of man for light with the sun to guide his steps and illumine his way—then why should he not meet the instinctive cry of our hearts that the beautiful Truths of his earthly life be preserved by something higher than the instinct of an animal or the erring reason of a human being or the light of a sun that sets?

Should not he who is Truth itself find a way to preserve that earth he has made, and the people he has made to rule it? I could never doubt the divinity of Christ after hearing his prophecies and learning of his miracles. There is only one thing that could make me doubt it, and that is that he should leave the earth without leaving the salt to preserve his Truth. If his own life could not be taken away from him by a crucifixion, how could we believe that his Truth, which is identical with that Life, could ever perish through the fickleness of human beings?

The means he left to preserve his truth, the channel to prolong his teaching, the instrument to communicate his voice often escapes us because of its simplicity. The means he chose are the same as those he chose to communicate it originally, namely, through a body with a head and living voice. When the Vicar of Christ, the successor of Peter, proclaims an infallible truth he does not make an absolutely new and personal pronouncement; he merely articulates and objectivates the mind of Christ.

The dominant note of the modern world is confusion. It has not only lost its way; it has even thrown away the map. It stands bewildered, lost, stunned, afraid to enthuse or even trust, lest its new love prove as unfaithful and as fickle as the others. It finds some solace for its bewilderment by repeating, "We must just go on experimenting, for we know not where we are going, or why we are here." But it is only for a moment. Each *con* has its *pro*, each *pro* its *con*. Every lunatic has his "case," every fool admits "another side," and every sphinx offers ten thousand answers to every ten thousand questions. When brought face to face with the certitude a Catholic has in his faith, or the peace of soul and security and the feeling of "being at home" a convert has in coming into the Church, the confused modern attributes it to excessive credulity, to the surrender of reason, to priest-craft—in a word, to anything and everything except the real reason, namely, the discovery of truth.

What are we asking for in the world today? The bankers' money? The power of kings? The plaudits of the mob? None of these things do we seek. What we are asking for, if we are honest with ourselves, is certainty—a tiny atom of unquestionable divine truth. We cannot live without it; we scan every eye, knock at every door, watch every lip, and fathom a thousand hearts, to catch but a ray of certainty and truth. Who among you have listened to the Babel of confusing voices, who have read the oldest and latest wranglings of prophets, who have turned an ear to inner voices, have found that truth that strikes you prostrate on the earth like a flash of divine lightning? Truth is what you seek: a belief that cannot be shaken; a knowledge that cannot be debated; a truth that lays hold so firmly on the mind that to conceive its opposite is impossible; a truth that is the last and most solid prop of reality—a truth that even is worth dying for!

And where is that truth? That Truth, which came to this world [two thousand] years ago is now living on earth today and speaking in a new body, the Church.

It is divine truth that makes the Church the stumbling block of the skeptics, the scandal of the half-hearted, the reproach of the ignorant. But no one escapes her, for they realize she stands on the crossroads of a drab civilization as the only rock of security and truth. From the outside, millions view her: some hate, some hesitate, some meditate. She gets in some people's hair; she gets in other people's brains—but she gets in *our hearts*!

Eight

Is Western Civilization Dying?

OUR WESTERN CIVILIZATION is the heir of the three master ideas: the value of the person, born of the Hebraic-Christian theology; the one-world and one-humanity concepts flowing from the baptized law of the Roman culture; and finally, our modern technology, which is the unfolding of the Grecian view of the autonomy of natural science.

Western civilization with its Christian roots is not perishing; it is beginning to come into its own. The spread of democracy throughout the world, the formation of new nations rooted in the respect for human persons, the embarrassment of Communist dictatorships at their failure to give free suffrage to their people—all these represent the leavening process of the cult of the value of the individual.

The reverence for the value of the person in history is evident in the contrast between the building of pyramids and the building of cathedrals. Pyramids were built on the backs of slave labor, but cathedrals were elevated by persons with master ideas. Instead of the contempt for persons which permeated the works of the ancient cities, in the West, the artisan, the architect, the sculptor, and the painter were accorded a dignity and full privilege as free citizens in the service of God. Max Weber has made this basic liberty of persons, which built history in the name of God, the basic differentiation between the Western and all non-Occidental cultures.

The gradual integration of nations into international bodies, such as the United Nations, the growing sense of responsibility that we are our brothers' keepers, foreign aid, the Peace Corps, missions—all these are the full-blown fruit of the baptized Roman concept of law as the juridical bond of all people. It was ancient Rome that gave law to the world, and it was the Christianized Latin culture that gave it international law.

Western civilization, instead of dying, is actually beginning to influence the world more than ever. In a magistral study of the East and the West, Arend Th. Van Leeuwen likens the influence of the non-Western world to a benign virus, which enters into the organism and makes it immune to further disease. It may also be compared to an injection of vitamins which gives strength to the organism. From another point of view, it is like a blood transfusion which strengthens the cells and gives the heart new life. Finally, it may also be compared to a catalyst which precipitates rapid changes and makes new combinations within a stable chemical structure. As Leeuwen puts it:

> There are quite a number of signs that the transformation which the non-Western world is undergoing is not a movement in just one particular direction, but is more like a large-scale process of fermentation, in which various extremely diverse and contradictory tendencies are involved. We see the non-Western religions parading as the champions of peace, and yet providing an ideological foundation in the struggle for political power.... It is in the West that a human society has been transformed into *the society par excellence*; and it is an extension of the West

that has made our world a planetary world, while it is again the West that has achieved the demotion of the earth to the status of a paltry planet.

This impact of the roots of Western civilization upon the world has been called secularization, which is distinct from secularism. Secularization is a process, a continuing historical *aggiornamento* of the spiritual leaven of the Hebraic-Christian tradition. Secularism, on the contrary, is an ideology or an attempt to find the cause, the origin, and the nature of man within the limitations of space and time. The Kingdom of God and the world are two correlative terms, the latter including the former, as the field includes the treasure: "The Kingdom of Heaven is like a treasure hidden in a field."

As centuries go on, the Church and the world are in mutual interaction. We leave out the fact of persecution but speak of the Church as an organizing principle of life, like the parable of the leaven and the mustard seed: The leaven in the mass of dough radiates its influence; the mustard seed in the earth absorbs energy from the earth and the air that surrounds it.

These are the two influences of the Kingdom of God in the world—namely, a diffusion of the Divine and the absorption of the cosmic and the human. There is nothing dramatic about the Kingdom of God in the world; it is not a sudden, violent upheaval but a silent, persistent process eventually reaching to the end of the earth. Secularization is nothing else than the two-thousand-year-old influence of Christianity, expressing and manifesting itself in love of neighbor. The flow of lay men and women will go across the world in various kinds of social service, with the deep conviction that God is calling them to witness to him in every aspect of life.

Nine

How to Be Missionary Though Ill

Which is nobler in the eye of God:
To be mission-ed to a bed of pain
Or to touch lepers in alien lands?
God has but one scale to judge which
  note is sweeter.
And that is the one who does His Holy Will.

When, then, all your fires are dying—
Too lame to march, too spent to spend
Your light on un-Gospeled lands
Put your soul at peace!

Did not David give the spoils of war
Not just to those who battled and besieged
But also to the ill who willed to fight
And could not?

Did not Paul from darkened prison-gloom
Boast that the Gospel prospered more in
  Caesar's lands
Than if he had been free of chains and bars?

If Gideon's few, smiting vessels of clay
Did disperse the massed Medianites' might
Then shall not your body, broken as
    so much clay,
Share in the mission of the Crucified:
"This is My Body—broken for you."

If broken loaves did feed a multitude
and broken alabaster announce
    the Friday-death,
If a broken net did token a great catch
And a broken roof admit palsied
    limbs to Christ,
And a broken ship save Paul and all
    who would be lost,
—Then shall not thy broken un-missioned life
Have, in God's eyes, the widest mission yet,
The mission of minting for those who go
The purchase price of souls?

You are the bread they consecrate,
The wine they bless;
Others may be on a Plastic Cross
But yours—like Christ's—is Wood.

Ten

The Christian Life

WHEN I AM ASKED what the Church means to me, I answer that it is the Temple of Life in which I am a living stone; it is the Tree of Eternal Fruit of which I am a branch; it is the Mystical Body of Christ on earth of which I am a member. The Church is, therefore, more to me than I am to myself; her life is more abundant than mine, for I live by union with her. She could live without me, for I am only a cell in her body; but I could not normally live without her. I live only as a part of her, as my arm lives only as a part of my body. So absorbing does she become that her thoughts are my thoughts; her loves are my loves; her ideals are my ideals. I consider sharing her life to be the greatest gift God has ever given to me, as I should consider losing her life the greatest evil that could befall me.

Dependence is the very essence of my creaturely existence, for no person is sufficient unto himself. I am not a speck in a moral void, nor a wanderer without a home, nor an isolated unit in creation. Rather, I am dependent on the God-appointed destiny whereby I *share* my love of God with others who love God in the unity of the Mystical Body of Christ. In that Body which is the fullness of Christ do I find the spiritual environment for my spiritual life. In her I live and move and have my being. From out her seven fountains I draw the waters of everlasting life. From out her book of the Seven Seals I learn the secrets of the Lamb. From out her tabernacles I draw the Bread of Life and the wine that germinates virgins. My life is her life; my being is her being. She has my love, my service, as I myself have the entire devotion and service of my hand. She is the living organism, but I am an organ. She is the body, but I am a member. She is Life, I am the living thing. She is the Spouse of Christ, I am but a feature. She is the Vine, and I am a branch.

> Abide in me, and I in you. As the branch cannot bear fruit of itself, unless it abides in the vine, so neither can you, unless you abide in me. I am the vine and you are the branches: He that abides in me, and I in him, the same bears much fruit: For without me you can do nothing (Jn 15:4–5).

We must not think, because the fullness of our spiritual life is in the Church, that she absorbs us and leaves no room for our individual development. Just as in the natural order the individual cell has its own growth even though it dwells in the body, so in like manner the individual Christian has his own personal development even though a member of the Mystical Body.

There is only one sun to shine upon all the flowers of the world, and hence all flowers are members of the kingdom of the sun. But their mutual dependence on the sun does not prevent the sun from drawing out of each flower its own particular beauty, and its own peculiar perfume. So does Christ in his dwelling in the Church give life and beauty to all who receive him, yet to each individual soul the Mystical Body gives its special life and beauty. So much so, that there is consummated under the bowers of the Church the union of the soul and its Divine Beloved, which death does not part but seals in everlasting bliss.

The body is made up of many members and countless

cells—each with its own personality, though all draw upon a common life and are animated by a common soul. There is no legitimate natural twist or bent or leaning of any personality in the world that cannot find its outlet in the organism of the Church.

While living his historical life our Blessed Lord did not destroy the personalities of his twelve apostles because they were one with him. Nor did he destroy the passion of a Magdalene after her conversion. He merely changed the direction of their inclinations, making them flow upward instead of downward, transforming an impetuous Simon to a daring Peter, a hating Saul into a loving Paul, a flesh-loving Magdalene into a spirit-loving Mary. Now that he has ascended into heaven and sent his Spirit into his Mystical Body the Church, he continues to draw all souls into the common life of that Body without destroying their property as a member or a cell of the Body.

The simple little girl of Lisieux did not cease to be a Little Flower because she became a Carmelite in the Mystical Body of Christ. Ignatius was a soldier both before and after he became the founder of the Jesuits. Louis IX was a king even though he was a subject of the King of Kings. And, in like manner, each and every one of us may continue to live our distinctly different lives in the office, in the field, at the machine, and at the university, in the humble duties of a routine world and in the lofty position as leaders of others, just as Thomas à Becket could wear the purple on the outside to please his people and the penitential chain on the inside to please himself.

There is no destruction of nature by grace, but only its elevation to another order. Tears are a common fountain for joy and sorrow. Passions, too, are common outlets for virtue and vice. It is not a different passion that makes a person a saint, from that which makes him a devil. It is the same passion going in a different direction. The Church, then, in embracing our lives within her common life does not destroy our personalities—she does not even destroy our most wicked passions. She transmutes them by the magic of her sacraments, provides new outlets, fixes new goals, and digs new channels.

The heroes of the world are not different from the martyrs. The same natural courage which would make a man die for Caesar on a battlefield, the Church would transmute into a supernatural courage which would make that person die for Christ. The bigots are all potential missionaries, for the same zeal that makes them unwittingly serve falsehood can be elevated by the Church to make them serve Divine Truth. The great scientists are all incipient theologians, for that same curiosity, which drives them to a knowledge of secondary causes, the Church transmutes by leading them to a knowledge of the First Cause which is God. We would not say that the hero who became a saint, nor the bigot who became a missionary, nor the scientist who became a theologian, lost their personalities once incorporated into Christ's Body, any more than we lost our personalities once we became citizens of a nation. But we would say that in their union with that common life of grace they had found the sublimation of their distinct personalities, and the crown of their individual selves. They would see, as we see, that Christ's Mystical Body is like a beautiful garden, formed by the blossoming of individual flowers each in its own beauty, but in its varied beauty blending into one harmonious, rapturous delight. Each flower of that garden has its own beauty revealed as in no other flower, yet each flower grows in beauty by contrast and by blending with the other flowers all rooted in a common soil and lighted by a common sun.

So it is in the mystical life, where Christ dwells in his Church, revealing himself anew in each individual soul, and never in two wholly alike—here manifesting himself in a Peter, there in a Paul, here in a Martha, there in a Mary, here in a lover of his infancy, there in a lover of his Cross, here in a rose with thorns, there in a flower without them, and yet all growing more beautiful by their fellowship with other saintly flowers because all rooted in the same Christ-life and all lighted by the same Christ-truth.

Eleven

First Come, Then Go

IT IS VERY LIKELY that priests who have been hearing confessions for many years have noticed a considerable change in the outlook of moral theology. Over twenty years ago, very few of us ever heard of sin against social justice. For example, "I pay an insufficient wage to my maid." Or, "My employees are underpaid." That was because there was an emphasis on the individual virtue, worth, and holiness, and a neglect of the social. Now we've gone to the other extreme. We have the emphasis on the social to the neglect of the individual. Very often you prove your religion today by carrying banners, by protests, by identifying with social programs, and there are some—particularly those who are given to the flesh—who think that if they are interested in social justice, immorality really does not matter very much.

Each of these extremes is wrong. And they are not only extremes in moral positions. It almost seems as if we have two kinds of Churches: one, the Church of evangelization; the other, the Church of development. One, the Church of individual sanctification, and the other that of social action. One, with emphasis on contemplation, and the other on political directives. And there is a division throughout the entire Western world regarding these two Churches. Is the division justified? Well, let us go to the Mount of Transfiguration for the answer.

Our Blessed Lord had just been to Caesarea Philippi and

had received from Peter the confirmation of his divinity; and now he takes with him Peter, James, and John to this mount. When they arrive our Blessed Lord now becomes transfigured. I wonder if that was not his "natural" state—divinity shining through a human nature was bound to radiate effulgence—so that it would seem he almost had to restrain this inner beauty from pouring out through the veil of his flesh. And he spoke with Moses and Elijah, the two who did not die. (Moses, it seems, did not. As a man of 120 or more, Moses climbed up the mountain and looked back to his people. All of them had tears in their eyes. Scripture says, "And no one knows the grave of Moses" (Deut 34:6). (He never got into the Holy Land, except after he died.) The Lord now speaks to the law and to the prophets. About what? About his death, his exodus. He speaks of passing from the Egypt of sin to the Promised Land, and he receives from his heavenly Father the renewal of his commission to redeem the world.

Peter, James, and John are awed by this. Peter, in fact, was so struck by this that he said, "Lord, it's wonderful to be here. Let us build three tabernacles: one for you, one for Moses, and one for Elijah." And Scripture says of Peter, "He knew not what he said." Now remember, here is the Church. Here are three members of the apostolic body. There's our Blessed Lord himself. Our Lord takes no part in the discussion, particularly with Peter. It's only the evangelist who knows Peter did not know what he was saying. This represents one Church. This represents those who would like everything to be rather calm, to enjoy the pieties and the niceties of religion, to stand in the glare of the divine beauty and be a sharer in the vision and the understanding of the Old Testament. And also to be "in," to be a part of the divine commission to redeem the world—even though it meant the death of the Savior. This is one aspect of the Church. It is apt to be the older aspect: content with the vision. But our Blessed Lord said, "Let us go down the hill." He was reminding them that there's no such thing as capturing that transient glory. You have to go down this hill and you'll find something else, and then you'll climb another hill, which will be Calvary. And then you will come to the perfect glory. *But not now.* So he takes them down the Mount of the Transfiguration.

Recall that great artistic work of Raphael, where two scenes are viewed together: the mountain scene depicting Christ in his glory, with the three disciples; and at the bottom, when the Lord comes down, a depiction of part of the Church—nine apostles, nine bishops, dealing with a social problem. Here we see a distraught father, with a boy who had a "mental" problem. Actually he is the symbol of any social problem and the symbol of any father's worry. And the father goes to the Church and asks, "Will you help this boy? This is not a religious problem that I have. It belongs in the social order. Heal him." When the Lord comes down and finds this other part of his Church, the father comes to our Lord and says, "They could not drive the devil out of my son. Will you drive him out?" And our Blessed Lord said to them, "How long must I suffer you?" This is the Church of development. This is the Church of social action; the Church of economic and political order; the Church of secularity. This is the Church of involvement, because the other was the Church of ecstasy and apart-ment—individual sanctification, joy, happiness, peace.

And they said, "Why cannot we drive the devil out?" Our Lord almost became intolerant of them. "Oh ye of little faith." *You have no faith! You were trying to build up a new world. That kind is driven out only by prayer and fasting.*

Which Church was right? Neither. And that's the modern world. Divide it as you please. Say the Church on the mountain represents the old; say the Church in the valley represents the young. It does not matter which. Both of them are ineffective. One's sleeping, misinterpreting the passion of Christ, trying to translate an emotion into a religion—like some "holy rollers" who make religion an emotional thing. And the other was dealing with the hard facts of life. So, this is our divorce. Neither one was right. If we are to build up a Church for this new age, we will have to begin by putting the two together. By returning to the very fundamental doctrine that "the Word became flesh." First, the spiritual. Then, the action. *Contemplata alias tradere.*

When Goethe's Faust was retranslating the Gospel of John, the devil could not translate that first line, "In the beginning was the Word" (he belonged to the second Church), and so what he said was "In the beginning was action." In the beginning was the deed. What was the first word of our Lord's public life? "Come." Come and see where I live.

We come to him, we catch fire, we absorb divine truth, we become filled with the Spirit, we begin to understand how the Eucharist is extended throughout the world in human flesh. And after we have come, then we learn the last word of our Lord's public life: "Go." *Go into the world.* Now we are prepared to go. Over the last many years we've had too many who "went" but who did not "come."

I once gave a day of recollection for Mother Teresa's community in New York and I asked the local pastor, who was one of the wisest men about social work that I ever talked to in my life—he had been in that locality for twenty-nine years—"How many apartment buildings in this area, those that are over five stories high, would you say are completely vacant and burned out?" And he answered, "between seventy and eighty percent." I then said, "What is your experience during these last ten, fifteen years?" "Well," he replied, "we had a number of priests and sisters who just flooded our area. They were going to reform everything.

They had to be involved. But they ran up against frustrations. Their theories didn't work out. Their idealism was defeated. They could not drive out any devils. And because they had no inner strength they all left." And then he said, "If they had had inner strength, if they loved Christ and the Cross, and the Blessed Sacrament, they could have taken it—as I have taken it. And as I love it."

There's no point, then, in holding workshops to discuss one or the other point of view, because the two must be put together. In the Gospel of Luke—that wonderful evangelist who was so human; the scribe of the neatness of Christ, he has been called—we have the story of the Good Samaritan, which Luke follows with the story of Martha and Mary. In other words, it's as if he is saying, "All right, you who read my gospel. You're going to care for all those wounded people that you pick up? And you're going to take them to a hospice? Fine. Read on. Do not become too busy. Otherwise you might be like Martha—preparing a Thousand Island salad, and gathering the salad from each of the Thousand Islands. You have to take time out to be like Mary and sit at the feet of Christ." This is the truth. Yet too often this is presented to us as a conflict of age groups: the young vs. the old. It is not a conflict of age groups any more than it was on the Mount of the Transfiguration. We cannot always remain on the mountain. We have to go down into the valley. There is the ecstasy, but there are also the problems; and the two have to be kept together.

In a world where we are so *overbusy*—that's the only way to describe it—we have to be fortified on the inside, not only by a sacrifice but by a sacramental presence. Then when we go out into the world we bring an entirely different view. Then we begin to see that there are three kinds of ills we have to deal with. First of all, there are handicaps—what the old Vulgate called the "thorn in the flesh." But that is not it. Actually, the Greek word used means a "stake." Saint

Paul had a *stake* impaled inside of him. What it was we do not know. It might have been an ailment of the eye, because he could not see well (he once struck a blind priest, and he said the Galatians would have given their eyes for him). But in any case, these are the "handicaps" that are imposed upon us on the inside—or better, perhaps, they come from the inside. The other kind of ill we have to deal with is a "burden." The burden does not come from within, such as Paul's eye trouble. The burden is thrust upon us. As the Cross was thrust upon Simon of Cyrene. "Come to me all you who are heavily burdened and find rest for your souls."

What is a "cross," and how does it differ from a "handicap" and a "burden"? A cross is either, but borne in the name of Christ. That's the Cross. With all the people we deal with in the world, regardless of what kind of problem they have—from within or without—what we have to do is always act in such a way as to enable them to see the relationship between their problem and the Cross.

I once asked Mother Teresa, who converted 15,000 men out of the gutters of Calcutta, "How, after dragging these poor mortals to your hospice, could you ever evangelize them and teach them the gospel?" And she said, "I didn't. When I took care of them and showed love, I would say to them, 'Would you like to hear about Christ?' And they would say, 'Is Christ like you?'" Mother Teresa would say, "No, but I try to be like him." "Then I want to be a Christian." It was that simple. That is the way *action* is to be done. So others will, without ever hearing a word from us, know about us and what we stand for. Like the old woman in the Book of Kings, who said to her husband, "The prophet passes here every day, he never says a word, he never preaches to us, but I know that he is a man of God. Just by his actions."

And that is why, when we stay close to the good Lord in the Blessed Sacrament, all the poor people whom we meet will come to see their flesh as the extension of the Body of

Christ. That outlook will come through to them. Then we will be Christians. Then we will not be on the mountain in ecstasy. Then we will not be in the valley impotent, ineffective. But we'll be the kind the world is looking for.

A group of Russian soldiers not too long ago broke into a barn in Russia and found a group of people in prayer and said, "You are violating Soviet law. Prayer is forbidden. We give you five minutes to leave. All who remain will be shot." Two left. The Russian soldiers threw down their guns and said, "We want to be Christians, too. We only wanted to be sure that *you* were *really* Christians."

Twelve

Is Religion Purely Individual?

HAVE YOU EVER HEARD anyone say, "I do not want any Church standing between me and God"? Do not be too harsh on them, for this statement is due to a misunderstanding. They would never say, "I do not want the United States government standing between me and America." To say I want no one between God and me is anti-Christian because it implies that your brother is a barrier to God's grace and not a means to it.

Did not our Blessed Lord say that before offering your gift at the altar, you should first go and reconcile yourself with the brother whom you offended, and then come and offer your gift? Did he not also make love of God absolutely inseparable from love of neighbor? Did he not teach us to pray in the context of "Our Father," not "My Father"; "our daily bread," not "my daily bread"; "our trespasses," not "my trespasses"? And if God is a father, then those united to him are brothers and sisters. Therefore, religion must be social.

We are not allowed individual interpretation of the Constitution of the United States. A Supreme Court does that for us. Why should someone insist on individual interpretation of religion and not begin all religious discussions with: "Now, this is what *I believe* about religion" or, "*I feel* this way about God"?

Never were the sublime and beautiful realities put so

much at the mercy of a stomach. Do you have your own individual astronomy and individual mathematics? Is not the personal pronoun "I" the most indecent of all the pronouns, and do you not dislike those people whose "I's" come too close together? Why, then, do you think the "I" used in isolation from your fellowmen is pleasing to God? Do not say, then, "religion is a private affair" any more than you would say your birth is a private affair. You cannot even die alone, for your death is tied up with property—or at least with burial. You cannot practice religion alone, any more than you can love alone.

What would happen to your patriotism if you said, "Patriotism is an individual affair"? If you were the only citizen in America, could you be patriotic? If you were the only person in a town, could you be charitable? If, then, you cannot be kind alone, or sacrificing alone, or generous alone, how in the name of God do you expect to be religious alone? As generosity implies a neighbor, as patriotism implies fellow citizens, so religion implies others with us in relation to God.

All the best things of life come from solidarity and fellowship. God said to hydrogen and oxygen, "Say 'Ours,'" and we have the oceans and tumbling cascades. The musician says to the scattered notes, "Say 'Ours,'" and we have the symphony. The sun says to the planets, "Say, 'Ours,'" and we have a planetary system. Your mind says to ideas and words, "Say 'Ours,'" and we have languages. America says to Americans, "Say 'Ours,'" and we have democracy. Even the animals that say "Ours" survive in the struggle of existence: the bees, the ants, and the birds. But those dinosaurs and ichthyosaurs who roamed in isolation and made living a private affair have perished from the earth.

Now ask yourself the important question: How do I contact Christ the Redeemer? How does he save me? How do I come to know his Truth and his Will? How do I receive his

Life? Do I contact him as an individual: by reading about him, and singing hymns to him, or do I contact him in fellowship and in community?

One way to answer that question is to inquire how humanity contacted God before the coming of Christ. Was religion a purely individual affair, or was it corporate? Did God deal with individuals directly, or indirectly, that is, through a race or a community?

Search the Scriptures. You will find that God always dealt with mankind through human corporations or races, or moral bodies, presided over by a divinely chosen head. The Book of Genesis reveals that the history of mankind would be a warfare not between individuals, but between two seeds, two races, two corporate wholes: the power of darkness and the power of light. "I will put enmities between thee and the woman, and thy seed and her seed; she shall crush thy head, and thou shalt lie in wait for her heel" (3:15).

The head of the corporation of evil was Satan; the invisible head of the corporation of good was God, but God always chose a visible head of that community to act in his name. First it was Noah, through whom and whose kindred salvation would come to humanity. Later, there came the new heads of this new spiritual corporation: Abraham, Isaac, and Jacob. To this community, God promised blessing and salvation. Later on, it was Moses whom God summoned as the head of his chosen people and through whom he promised their nation, "I will take you to myself for my people: I will be your God, and you shall know that I am the Lord your God, who brought you out from the work prison of the Egyptians" (Ex 6:7).

A covenant or contract was entered into between this community and God, in which God promised to bless them if they would obey his law and become his faithful witnesses and the bearers to the world of the Messiah, the "Expected of the Nations," the Savior of the world. After Moses, there were Joshua, David and the prophets.

God always followed the same method. He never communicated his promises to individuals in the world at large, but to his chosen people through some chosen patriarch, or leader, or king, or prophet.

Whenever God willed to give new or special privileges to the community, he changed the name of his head, for example, Abraham, Jacob. This corporation, or chosen body, was not always faithful; it sometimes fell into idolatry, but despite their lapses, God was with them as his instrument— guiding, controlling, directing, so that in whatever they did his purpose never failed.

It was always the chosen community or moral body, and not the individual, which received God's revelation. Very likely, at the time of the flood, every individual might have liked to have his personal rowboat, but God saved them in an ark under his own divinely appointed captain.

Throughout Jewish history, the community always holds first place, and the greatest punishment that could be inflicted upon any individual Jew was to be cut off from his corporate body. Even today, to the Orthodox Jews, the most serious of all sanctions is, in our modern language, "to be put out of the synagogue," which, it will be recalled, was done to Spinoza.

So it came to pass that the most important word in the Old Testament was the word that expresses this corporation, or body, or congregation, or society. That word was *kahal*. About two hundred years before Christ, the Jews translated their Scriptures into Greek because so many Jews were living away from Israel in a Greek civilization. When the translators came to the Jewish word *kahal*, they translated it by the Greek work *ecclesia*, which means "that which is called out," signifying that its members had been called out from the secular nations.

When finally the Messiah did come in the person of Christ Jesus, true God and true man, it was only natural to expect that God would now continue to deal with mankind in much the same way that he dealt with it before, namely, through a corporation presided over by a head whom he himself would choose.

An *ecclesia* was already in existence when "God sent his Son, made of a woman, made under the law" (Gal 4:4). Our Lord was born in the very heart of a divinely chosen community or *ecclesia*. God who in previous times spoke through the prophets now would speak through his Son to give the fullness of revelation.

Now that the fullness of time was come, God willed to elevate his *ecclesia* to the fullness of truth, power, and grace. As once before he had named Abraham, Moses, and David as its head, so now he would name someone else as its head. Because new powers and privileges were to be given, he changed the name of that individual. As he changed Abram's name to Abraham, Jacob's name to Israel, so now he changed the name of the individual who is to be the new head, from Simon to Rock. In English, his name is Peter. We lose the flavor of it in English because Peter and Rock are different words. But they are not so in the language our Lord spoke—nor in French, Greek, Latin, and several other languages. For example, in French Pierre means Rock and it is also the name of a man. In the original Greek, our Lord said, "Thy name is Simon: Henceforth thou shalt be called the Rock."

On that day, when the Rock confessed that Christ was the Son of the Living God, the Divine Master answered, "Thou art Peter; and upon this rock I will build my church, and the gates of hell shall not prevail against it." From now on God's *ecclesia* would be built upon the Rock, and it would be to the whole world God's chosen community for the communication of his Divine Life, as Israel before had been the community for the communication of his promise.

No wonder the Rock, in his first sermon on Pentecost, spoke of the continuity of God's plan, namely, that "those things which God before had shown by the mouth of all the prophets, that his Christ should suffer, he hath so fulfilled" (Acts 3:18) "by the hands of wicked men," but nonetheless in accordance with his "determinate counsel and foreknowledge" (Acts 2:23).

Our Lord said this new *ecclesia* would start small, like a mustard seed, but it would grow into a great tree, "so that the birds of the air may dwell under the shadow thereof" (Mk 4:32). It would be a new society with other ideals, purposes, and goals than the world; hence, it would be hated by the world as he was hated. Its members would be so closely united to one another and in him, that if anyone did a kind act to any other member—for example, give him food or a drink of cold water—they would be doing it for him. The unity between him and it, he said, would be like the unity between the vine and its branches.

This new *ecclesia* or body was, therefore, not to be like a club which is formed by individuals coming together to a center for a common purpose. Rather, it was to be like a living body, from whose center life radiates until the organism is made perfect. It would not be people who would make a contribution to his organization; it would be him who would fill them with life.

The nucleus of this *ecclesia* was the apostles, who were destined to spread out over the world, teaching all nations even to the consummation of the world. To this new *ecclesia* he promised to communicate his truth, his power, and his redemption which he had exercised through his physical body.

After all, was the truth he taught to be limited to his time, his generation? Was his power to be confined to those who saw his hands? Was his sanctification to be narrowed to those who climbed to Calvary? That people of his time might have no advantage over us, he gave to this new Body, or *ecclesia,* his truth, his power, and his sanctification. "I am the truth," (Jn 14:6) he said. But that truth he communicated to his *ecclesia:* "He that hears you, hears me; and he that despises you, despises me; and he that despises me, despises him that sent me" (Lk 10:16). When, therefore, this new *ecclesia* began to teach, it would be he who was teaching through them, just as he once taught through his human nature.

The Body of Christ is not only an organization, then; it is more like an organism. It no more stands between you and Christ than his physical body would have stood between you and his forgiveness. It was through his human body that he came to us on earth; it is through his Mystical Body, or *ecclesia,* that he comes to us now.

If anyone is surprised to hear that Christ, who is at the right hand of the Father with the glorified human nature, is now the Head of the new body of regenerated humanity, which has been growing since the day of Pentecost, and through which his truth is still preached, his authority still exercised, and his forgiveness still applied, recall the story of Paul's conversion, which took place a few years after the Ascension.

This fiery Hebrew of the Hebrews grew up with an unholy hatred of Christ and things Christian, and as a young man he held the garments of those who stoned Stephen, the first Christian martyr. Paul was not just a bigot. He was a learned man, trained under Gamaliel, so powerful a disputant that the early Christians must often have wondered after the death of Stephen whom they could find to refute him.

In the providence of God, it was reserved that Paul should refute a Paul. One day, he set out on a journey for Damascus, authorized by letters to seize the Christians of that city, bind them, and bring them back to Jerusalem. Breathing out hatred against the Lord, he departed to persecute the new infant *ecclesia*. Suddenly a great light shone about him and he fell to the ground, aroused by a voice like a bursting sea: "Saul, Saul, why do you persecute me?" Nothingness dared to ask the name of Omnipotence: "Who are you, Lord?" And he answered, "I am Jesus whom you persecute" (Acts 9:4–5).

Saul was about to strike the body of believers in the city of Damascus in exactly the same way that Christ's followers are persecuted in certain cities of the world today—and the Voice from heaven says, "Saul, Saul, why do you persecute me?"

Christ and his *ecclesia* are the same. The risen Christ, only four or five years after he had left this earth, broke open the heavens to declare to Paul and the world that in striking his Body you strike his Head, that the branches and the Vine are one; that, when the Body of the Church is persecuted, it is Christ who arises to speak. No wonder that the transformed and converted Saint Paul understood Christ as well as the other apostles, for he, too, had touched his Body.

Now we come to the answer to the question: How does Jesus save me? He saves me through his Body, or *ecclesia*, with this difference: his Body now is not physical, but mystical! It is made up of human natures infused with Divine Spirit. The only way in which we can be linked to another age is through a body of human beings, a body which, something in the manner of a natural body, renews itself through time.

The America of today is continuous with the America of Washington and Lincoln, through the body of government. Social clubs, baseball clubs, and steel corporations do not have the same membership now as ten decades ago, but they have maintained their continuity for generations through new members.

Likewise, the Body of Christ, the *ecclesia*, that exists today is continuous with him—through the members who have lived through time. Since Christ is the true God as well as true man, he should be able to do what no human being has ever been able to do, namely, to project his life, his truth, his love to the very doors of our day and to the very threshold of our hearts. Then, those who lived in his times should have no advantages in love and forgiveness over those who live in our times. If he is not the Eternal Contemporary, he is not God.

No single drop of blood can exist apart from your body, but your body can exist without that single drop of blood. So the Body of Christ can live without you, but you cannot live without the Body of Christ.

Thirteen

Zeal for Souls

THE GREAT CHARACTERISTIC of life is growth. Youth and growth are synonymous; age and decay are synonymous. Life has therefore been properly defined as the sum of those forces which resist death. The law of growth was imposed on creation when God told man and the lower creatures of which he was the master, "Increase and multiply." The same law of growth was imposed on supernature, on the Church, when our Lord told his apostles, "Preach the gospel to every creature." The Church was thus ordered to reproduce, to generate new life, to fill up the Kingdom of God, to make conquests from the outside, to increase progeny from within. For the Church that does not reproduce, that is not missionary, is weaving its own shroud. "You have not chosen me," said our Lord, "but I have chosen you; and have appointed you, that you should go, and should bring forth fruit, and your fruit should remain."

But just how is this Mystical Body of Christ to grow from a mustard seed into a great tree? Is it to grow by God pouring out his grace on human beings, while we the members remain inactive? Or is it to grow by members cooperating with the grace of God?

The laws of nature suggest the answer. The human body develops from infancy to perfection, thanks principally to food and drink. But food and drink would not make the body grow unless the body already possessed a soul, which is the principle of life. Corpses do not grow, regardless of how much nourishment is poured into them. Neither does the soul alone suffice for life. The food that the living body needs comes to the body through the members of the body: the feet that walk to the table and the hands that touch it and take it into the organism. Thus two factors combine for growth: the living soul, and the food given to the body through the help of the body itself.

The Church's soul is the Spirit of Christ, without which the Church would be an organization, not an organism. Its body is made up of all who have been baptized. But the Body and Soul alone are not enough to account for the growth of the Church. The Church, like the human body, depends for its development on the activity of its members. The fact that we share the life of Christ does not dispense us from the obligation of working with him for the increase of his Mystical Body. Do not the branches reach out to absorb the sunlight; do not the hands and feet reach out to grasp the food? Why then should not our Lord, in like manner, make the growth of his Church dependent on its members? Mary was called to share in the Redemption, and the apostles were called to preach what Christ had preached, and Peter was called to be the rock of his Church. In fact, since the call of Abraham and the endowing of Adam with free will, it is by means of human beings that God deals with everyone.

As the diamond is polished only by the diamond, so it is by and through human natures that Christ spreads the Kingdom. The zealous souls, the apostles, the missionaries in far countries, the saintly souls in our own land, the sisters in our schools, the priests in our parishes: All Christ-loving men and women whose hearts are on fire with the love of God, are the eyes, the feet, and the hands of Christ which reach out to the pagan, the dejected, the forlorn, the humanists, the sinners, the erring, to lift them into the Body where they may be quickened again into Life and Love and Truth by the vivifying power of the Spirit of Christ.

What nobler work could there be than zeal for souls? What finer way to spend oneself and be spent than in drawing souls to the love of their Lord and their God? The world holds in high repute physicians who restore health to the diseased, surgeons who amputate cancerous growth, teachers who bring history and grammar to the illiterate, social workers who rehabilitate the broken human earthenware of our streets, and scientists who extend the frontiers of our science beyond another star. All this is noble, but since there is a life beyond this one, let it be remembered that in the Book of Life they are written in letters of gold who do for souls what others have done for the body. The great Heart of Christ holds in eternal love *spiritual* physicians, *spiritual* teachers, *spiritual* surgeons—those who bring to others his truth, knowledge, healing, and grace.

The responsibility to extend the Mystical Body devolves upon every one of us. Any member who refuses the right of way to life by denying it facilities for transmission is guilty of a breach of trust. The privilege of being a cell in the Body is the privilege of a stewardship of service and of apostolate. Through loyalty to this missionary imperative each member may pay his debt of thanks for the gift of faith by endowing the future with that faith. Every living unit thus stands between past and future with obligations to both which it cannot default. What we have received we must pass on, not pocket. What has been given to us must not be confined, but cradled for growth. As guardians of the Divine Life that has come down to us since Pentecost, we must answer to God for misappropriation and impounding to our own ends. Every talent received must bear interest, and every grace received must furnish a highway along which the Gospel shall have a straight and unimpeded path for propagation.

We do not save our souls alone, but only in conjunction with others.

Fourteen

It Is Expedient That I Go

"IT IS EXPEDIENT to you that I go." The words of our Savior on the night before he died. Strange words, indeed!

Why should they be spoken at a moment when he had weaned the hearts of his apostles away from their nets, boats, and custom tables, and had entwined them so closely about his own Sacred Heart? How could it be expedient for them that he go? How could it be expedient for men who were wanderers on the sea of life that their Captain should be taken from them? How could it be expedient for them to be left alone at a moment when he was sending them out as sheep among wolves? How could it be expedient for men who lived so close to the material and the sensible to have him whom they once had seen and touched become the Great Unseen and Untouchable? And yet it was expedient for us that he go—otherwise he would not have told us so. Perhaps we can see reasons why it was expedient that he go.

First of all, if he had continued his earthly life to our own day, then the most important questions of life would have been left unanswered. Where does a good life lead? What is the reward for virtue? What lies beyond the tomb? Does a saintly life purchase anything better in the next world? Has heaven any crown for those who, like good shepherds, lay down their lives for their sheep? Certainly if Jesus has not merited eternal glory because of his earthly life, then wherein lies the value and the worth of anyone's good earthly life? Did not our Lord himself tell us that "it was fitting that the Son of Man should suffer in order that he might enter into his glory"?

In other words, one reason why it was expedient for our Lord to go was to show that the reward of a worthy life is not an earthly one—that each and every one us has an appointed task to do in this world, that we were sent into it to work out our salvation, and that when that task is accomplished and that work is done, like him we must press onward to our "supernal vocation," which is everlasting glory with him in heaven.

But it was expedient for him to go for still another reason: in order that he might be nearer to us. This is the very reason he gave for his going:

> [F]or if I go not, the Paraclete will not come to you; but if I go, I will send him to you.... But when he, the Spirit of truth, is come, he will teach you all truth...he shall glorify me; because he shall receive of mine, and shall show *it* to you.... A little while, and now you shall not see me; and again a little while, and you shall see me: because I go to the Father.... I will see you again, and your heart shall rejoice; and your joy no man shall take from you (Jn 16:7; 13–14; 16–18; 22).

In these solemn words spoken on the eve of his crucifixion he explicitly stated that he was going back to the boundless depths of his Father's life whence he came, but his going would not leave them orphans, for he would come again in a new way; namely, by his Spirit. Our Lord was equivalently saying that if he remained on earth in his physical life, he would have been only *an example to be copied*; but if he went to his Father and sent his Spirit, then he would be *a life to be lived*.

If he had remained visibly and tangibly with us, he would have been related to us merely as a model is related to the artist who chisels his marble, but never as the idea and inspiration that produces the work of art. If he remained on earth he would have been merely the subject of prolonged observation, of scientific study and imitation. But however noble his example, however inspiring his words, he would always have been *outside us, external to us*; an external voice, an external life, an external example—he could never be possessed other than by an embrace. The very physical body which housed that Divine Life would have been an obstacle to our loving him by a unity of mind, heart, and soul to which all true love must tend. If he had tarried on earth, all would have stood still. It would have been the perpetual promise of a day; a lingering blossom, a retarded fruit, a lengthening childhood, a backward maturity.

But by ascending to heaven to sit in glory at the Father's right hand, he could send his spirit into our souls. Thus he would now be with us not as an external person, but as a living soul. He would be not just a mere something mechanical to be copied, but a something vital to be reproduced, not a something external to be portrayed in our lives, but a something living to be developed within us. His Ascension into heaven and his sending of his Spirit alone makes it possible for him to unite himself wholly with us, to take up his abode with us—body and blood, soul and divinity—and to be in the strictest sense of the term "Christ in us."

The greatest joys in life are those that come from unity— the unity of citizens in a nation, the unity of children and parents in a family, the unity of interests and ideals among friends, and the unity of two in one flesh in the sacrament of matrimony. But even this last kind of unity, which is the deepest in the natural order because it bears fruit in a child, is still quite imperfect. The unity of the flesh need not always mean unity of the souls. Sometimes the possession of another outwardly is the greatest obstacle to inward possession. We never reach the height of unity until there is a fusion of loves, thoughts, and desires, a unity so profound that we think with the one we love, love with the one we love, desire what our beloved desires. And this unity is found in its perfection when the soul is made one with the Spirit of Christ which is the Spirit of God. The joys that come from human friendships, even the noblest, are but the shadows and fond reflections of the joy of a soul possessed of the Spirit of Christ.

What Christ did in his own human nature in Galilee, he is doing today in other human natures in New York, London, Paris, and every city and hamlet of the world where there are souls vivified by his Spirit. He is still being born in other Bethlehems of the world, still coming into his own and his own receiving him not, still instructing the learned doctors of the law and answering their questions, still laboring at a carpenter's bench, still "going about doing good," still preaching, governing, sanctifying, climbing other Calvaries, and entering into the glory of his Father.

There are poor people today in our bread lines, there are innocent people in our prisons, there are half-clothed families in our tenements, who are as ragged and destitute on the outside as they are rich with the Spirit of Christ on the inside. Externally they appear to most of us like the ordinary poor who attack the rich, like the common captive who harangues authority, like the selfishly needy who curse their lot, but the resemblance is only on the outside—and so many are deceived.

Some eyes are so filled with the dust of the world's traffic that they cannot see the divine grace in their own souls. The world classifies these in their social surveys as the poor, the dependent, the captive—but in the eyes of the Father in heaven they are other Christs in other deserts, thirsty at other Jacobs' wells, suffering on their crosses, captive in other praetoriums. The world sees them as so many economic problems; the heavenly Father sees them as beloved sons and daughters in whom he is well pleased.

This truth, that the Spirit of Christ dwells in the just, escapes the world. We know our Lord said it, we confess it with our lips, we believe it in our heart, but we do not seize it in *all* its reality. Not even the just and saintly Christians realize it as they should, and on Judgment Day even they will be surprised that Christ walked the earth again in those who were filled with his Spirit. ("Amen I say to you, as long as you did it to one of these my least brethren, you did it to me.")

It *was* expedient, therefore, that he go. Otherwise, he would have belonged to history and to a country. Now he belongs to us.

Fifteen

When We Suffer

When we suffer, we do not want one
Who stands over us like a physician,
Who touches us as tongs touch hot coals,
Who washes in antiseptic after contact,
And who parrots, "Keep your chin up."

We want One who left footprints
In the dark forest—so we can follow.
A Surgeon Who before He cuts
Says, "I had the same—see My scars!"
Someone Who stumbled to a Throne
And walked not unfallen to the Hill.

We want One Who, as we question,
"Does God know what it is to suffer?"
Can point to riven side and open heart
Saying, "Would you not be nobler than I
If you could suffer for Love,
And I could not?"

Yes! Christ is Judge. But until that
Great Assize when heaven's ledgers
are brought forth
He says, "I sentence you to death—
But I shall pay the penalty
And let you free."

Jesus is not just your Exemplar
As the model to the canvas.
He is not like oil on your baptismal water,
But like a blood transfusion in your veins,
Like the sunlight dancing in a stained-glass Gothic,
Like the fragile glass that breaks in sympathy
With the vibrant chords of a twin harmony.

He does not send your pain;
He sends it to Himself,
As the mother tastes the bitter draught
Before passing it to childish lips.

So long as you think of Christ outside your aches,
As the book of consolation that you read,
Or the healing medicine on the shelf,
You will never be a part of the saving Cross.

Does not even the gutter's stained drop
Reflect the brightness of the distant sun,
And is not its inner self lifted to the sun
Leaving only the scum behind?

In some such way,
Those whose pains are like moisture
Are absorbed into the world's redemption
And those whose hearts are as mud
Only harden with the fires of love.

We all weep that Jesus had no inn,
But today, does not Jesus weep
Because so few give Him neither inn nor Cross?

Jesus is never off His Cross!
He left it not in challenge:
"Come down! We will believe."

But what is harder than to hang there
Is to believe that He hangs on *me*.

Sixteen

Personality: Earth and Heaven

THERE HAS ALWAYS BEEN throughout human history a belief that the world, and all that is in it, is wicked. Oriental philosophies insisted on the extinction of desires. In Christian history one of the greatest of all heresies was Manicheanism—namely, that there was an absolute principle of evil working in the world, hence, not all creation is good.

Teilhard de Chardin sought to bridge this gap between the world and God, or between physics and theology, as Saint Francis before had bridged the gap between the Divine and the human. Francis found all humanity lovable; Teilhard found the cosmos lovable. As all mortals, even the weakest, told Francis of God, so the physical universe told Teilhard of the Divine. His background, he said, prepared him for seeking the union of the two:

> By education and intellectual training, I belong to the children of heaven. But by temperament and through my professional studies, I am a child of the earth. Placed thus by life at the heart of two worlds whose theory, language, and feelings I know, and because of intimate experience, I have not erected any inner partition in my mind…. Now at the end of this process, after thirty years dedicated to the pursuit of inner unity, I have the impression that a syn-

thesis has taken place naturally between these two currents which had been making contrary demands upon me. The one has not killed the other. Today I probably believe in God more than ever before—and certainly I believe more than ever in the world.

On October 7, 1946, he wrote that all his thought was in one direction: "a rethinking of Christianity on the scale and dimensions of the universe as it is revealed ever more clearly to us."

What Chardin strove to do was to avoid the dichotomy and the divorce between revelation and science, the commitment to the eternal and the commitment to the temporal, between loving God and loving the world.

Having lived many years of his life in a non-Christian civilization, he saw a vast civilized humanity growing up outside of the consciousness of Christ. This to him was not exclusively a tragedy; it was merely a summons for a new type of Christianity, which would be, at one and the same time, more involved in the world and more detached from the world. As he wrote, "The saint is the man who Christianizes in himself all that is human in his own time." He felt great pity "for those who live only for their own times and whose love extends no farther than their own country."

As one looks at the various trends in our day, one sees that Teilhard's conception of spirituality is in the forefront. He knew that he had to pass through many hazards, but his was directed principally to the cosmic world. Others have been directed to the human world. This does not mean to say that Teilhard limited himself to anthropology and physics. His fundamental orientation was "to attain heaven through the fulfillment of earth, [to] Christify matter."

It is very likely that when all the trivial, verbal disputes about Teilhard's "unfortunate" vocabulary will have died away or have taken a secondary place, Teilhard will appear, like John of the Cross or Saint Teresa of Ávila, as a spiritual genius of the twentieth century.

Teilhard was concerned not only with the outside of things, but with their "withinness." All reality has an inner face and an outer face. This withinness is difficult to detect the farther one goes back to primitive forms of life and to matter. But the more it becomes complex, the more it is observable. Just as families go to pieces without love, so the universe could also disintegrate and dissolve with the drawing of the Omega.

What Teilhard has done is to break with the sharp dualism between matter and consciousness, which was introduced into philosophy by Descartes. For Teilhard, there is a continuity between an animal seeking food and a magnet pointing to the north; between a male and female uniting in the act of generation and two atoms uniting to form a chemical compound. The meaning is not the same in each instance, but there is more than a mere figure of speech in this unification. Atoms are not alive, it is true, but they have what might be called prelife.

What, then, is evolution? It is not a sudden appearance of life and consciousness and sensitivity, but an elaboration, an organization, a centering of something *which was there inchoately from the beginning.* This Alpha-Omega is Christ, "in whom we live and move and have our being."

Humanity is the final result of the clustering and synthesizing of all the labors of the universe; in mankind consciousness becomes self-consciousness, related to the lower forms but transcendent to them. In all things there is an outside and an inside, a within and a without, or what scholastics call matter and form, wherein the world is charged with the grandeur of God. In Teilhard's vision of the universe, "No evolutionary future awaits man, except in association with all other men. Invention, communication, international politics all demand greater unity out of this multiplicity. Humanity is facing, therefore, either brotherly unity or atomic disintegration."

Thanks to communications, education, global network of trade and exchange, men and nations are weaving a pattern of greater and greater interdependence. This vast globality of common effort is what Teilhard calls the noosphere. Humanity is now at the crossroads of collective life or collective death. If it is to survive, what energy was to the lower order love must be to the human—namely, the drive to more and more complex social unity. And this is possible, because at both the beginning and the end of the whole evolutionary process, there is Love. The Love-point at the beginning which makes everything turn from complexity to unity is the Alpha; the goal toward which all tends is the perfect Love, or the Omega. As Teilhard wrote in *The Divine Milieu:*

> One day, the Gospel tells us, the tension gradually accumulating between humanity and God will touch the limits prescribed by the possibilities of the world. And then will come the end. Then the Presence of Christ, which has been silently accruing in things, will suddenly be revealed—like a flash of light from pole to pole.

Teilhard's thoughts were cosmic, human, and *Christic.*

Seventeen

The Spiritual Bethlehem

IN ADDITION TO the Church, by which Christ prolongs his Incarnation in his Mystical Body, something must be said of the role played by his Blessed Mother in that new Body. This is because her importance is such that it deserves a special consideration.

Some dim suggestion and hint of the part Mary plays in the regeneration of the human race is to be found in the part Eve played in its fall. Sacred Scripture tells us that Christ is the second Adam who, by his obedience on the tree of the Cross, undid the disobedience of the first Adam under the tree of knowledge of good and evil. If Christ is the spiritual counterpart of Adam and the new head of the human race, then Mary, the mother of those who live in Christ, is the counterpart of Eve, the mother of those who died in Adam. A fitting parallel, indeed, for if woman played such an important role in the fall of the human race, it is fitting that her role be no less important in its redemption. In a word, Mary is the Mother of the Mystical Body of Christ, the Church.

In order to understand how literal and real this truth is, dwell for a moment on the primary fact that Mary is the Mother of Christ. He who from all eternity was begotten of the Father is generated in terms of the Blessed Mother without man, but by the overshadowing of the Holy Spirit. Her life from that point on is inseparably bound up with his;

never does Scripture mention her apart from him. She is with her Divine Son in the flight to Egypt; she is with him in the temple praying the perfect prayer to the heavenly Father; she is with him during his labors and years of obedience in the humble Nazarene home; she is with him in his preaching, and stands at the foot of the Cross as he dies for the redemption of the world.

Such beautiful devotion makes her the loveliest of all the lovely mothers of the world, the paragon of maternity, and the prototype of motherhood. But this does not tell the whole truth concerning Mary. She was more than the mother of the physical Christ. If her divine Son were only a man, then her maternity might be purely a corporal one. But recall that her Son is the Son of God as well as the Son of Man. Recall, furthermore, that during his earthly life he promised to assume a new body after his Ascension into heaven, a body that would be made up of the countless faithful who believed in him, and through which body would flow his life and truth and love, like the sap of the vine flows through the branches. Once he ascended into heaven it was no longer possible for his physical body to grow and develop, for it possessed the fruits of glory. But the other body that he assumed on Pentecost, which is his Church, *could* grow like the mustard seed, and Saint Paul, building on that thought, speaks of it as the "increase of God."

This means that in addition to the physical Christ, whose life began at Bethlehem and ended with the Ascension, there is also the mystical Christ, which began with Pentecost and which will endure through all eternity. Now if the fullness of Christ embraces not only his historical life in Galilee, but also his mystical life in the Church, then should not Mary be not only the Mother of the physical Christ but also the Mother of the Fullness of Christ, the Mother of the Church? The mother of Jesus Christ, therefore, should be our mother, otherwise the whole Christ would not be entirely the son of

Mary. She would be his mother in the physical sense, but she would not be his mother in the mystical sense. She would be the mother of the Head, but she would not be the mother of his Body.

This could hardly be, for the sun that shines on the vine to give it strength also gives strength to the branches; thus it must be that she who is the Mother of the Vine, which is the natural Christ, is also the Mother of the Branches, which are the Church. As the Mystical Body is the complement and fullness of the natural Body of Christ, so too the Divine Motherhood of the Head should be complemented and have its fullness in the Motherhood of the Mystical Body. Since she cooperated in the Incarnation by her consent, she should also cooperate in the prolongation of the Incarnation: the Church.

Would there not be a great lack in what we receive from our Divine Savior if he had not also given his mother to us? Think of all the other heavenly benefits he gave us, and then ask yourself why he should stop short of giving us as mother the woman whom he chose above all the women of the earth as the Spotless Portal of the flesh through which he came to us in the form and image of ourselves. If his mother were not given, he has not been the Perfect Lover who gives all.

Would we not be orphans without a mother? If he emptied his generous heart by giving us his Father, his life, his Spirit, then why should his arm be shortened in holding back his mother? He called us to be his brothers and sisters, adopted sons and daughters of the heavenly Father. But if he has a mother, should not we who are his brothers also have the same mother? Grace is the perfection of nature, and if in the natural order we receive natural life through a woman, why shouldn't we also receive supernatural life? Once granted that he has given us his mother as our mother, then how true ring his words, "All my things are yours, and you are mine." What we would expect him to do as befitting his

Divine Love, he has actually done. Note how Sacred Scripture, at first implicitly, and then explicitly, reveals how Mary is the Mother of the Church. Recall that Saint Luke, in recounting the birth of our Lord, says that Mary brought forth her "first born." Certain critics have argued that this meant Our Lady had other children according to the flesh, quite ignoring the fact that the Scriptures clearly indicate she was a virgin. The phrase "first born" may indeed mean that Mary was to have other children, but not by the flesh, only by the Spirit. It suggests that she was to have a spiritual progeny which would make up the Mystical Body of her Divine Son, just as Eve is called the "mother of all living," to designate her as the mother of humanity in the natural order. Sarah gave only one son to Abraham, the father of believers, and yet she is called the Mother of all Israel.

So there is a clear suggestion in the words "first born" that she who begot corporally the Head of the Church was also to beget spiritually its members. Since the Head and the Body are inseparable, it is therefore true to say that when Mary bore Christ in her womb she was virtually carrying the whole Mystical Body. This mother who bears the vine also bears the branches.

Ten days after the Ascension we find the apostles "persevering with one mind in prayer with Mary the Mother of Jesus," awaiting the descent of the Holy Spirit. The Spirit had descended upon her at Nazareth to make her the Mother of Jesus; now he descends upon the apostles to make them his new Body and Mary the Mother of that Body. Virgin in the flesh, she brought forth her first born, Christ; virgin by the purity of her faith, she brings forth her other-born, the Church—and in both instances it is the Holy Spirit that renders her fecund.

Such was God's reason for leaving the Blessed Mother on earth for a time after her Son had ascended into heaven.

Called to the sublime vocation of being the Mother of Christ in his redemptive work, it was her duty not only to cradle the Head of the Church in Bethlehem, but also to cradle the Body in Jerusalem. The Mystical Body of Pentecost, like the physical body of Bethlehem, was small and delicate and frail, like any newborn thing. Its members were small; its organs were in the process of formation, and though life was there it was yet to grow in "age and grace and wisdom before God and men." But that growth and development could not be without the menace of hatred and persecution; for the new Herods would arise to attack the Church as the other Herod had attacked its Head.

It was necessary, therefore, that the Mother of the infant Mystical Christ be there to bestow her loving care on it, as thirty-three years earlier she had watched over the infant Christ. Every infant needs a mother's care—even an infant Church. The mystery of Jesus did not begin without her; neither would it finish without her. Our Blessed Lord had kept his promise. He did not leave us orphans.

Not only was it fitting that Mary be present as mother at the birth of the Mystical Christ, it was also fitting that she be present as Queen of the Apostles on the solemn day when the Church began preaching the gospel to the world.

From the very beginning she was the apostle *par excellence* of her Divine Son. She it was who first made Jesus known to his precursor John the Baptist on the occasion of her visit to Elizabeth; she it was who first made Jesus known to the Jews in the persons of the shepherds, and to the Gentiles in the persons of the Wise Men. It was therefore in keeping with her vocation that she be with the apostles on Pentecost to make known the Mystical Christ to the world, as she had made known the physical Christ to shepherds and kings. She gave birth to him, who came to cast fire on earth and willed that it be enkindled, and her role would now have been incomplete if she had not been in the very center of the tongues of fire which the Spirit of her Son sent upon the apostles to make them burn with his message even to the consummation of the world.

Pentecost was Mary's spiritual Bethlehem, her new Epiphany in which, as mother, standing by the crib of the Mystic Christ, she makes him known once again to other shepherds and other kings.

Finally, when in the providence of God the Church had grown to its full stature and begun its "public life," as her Son began his when he left the maternal home in Nazareth, Mary was called home to her reward. Her Divine Son had his crucifixion and Resurrection and then his Ascension. Mary had her crucifixion as the sword of sorrow pierced her heart on Calvary. But she was now to have the counterpart of his Ascension—and that was her Assumption into heaven.

In that state of glory for which we labor here below, Christ the Head of the Mystical Body lives to intercede for us before the heavenly Father. Associated with him in glory, as she had been associated with him in his earthly pilgrimage, is his Mother, the Queen of Angels and Saints. Inseparably united at the Cross when the reservoirs of redemption were filled, they are now inseparably united in heaven as those same merits are poured out upon all who believe in him as Brother, in her as Mother, and in God as Father.

It is impossible to love Christ adequately without also loving the Mother who gave him to us. Those who begin by ignoring her soon end by ignoring him—for the two are inseparable in the great drama of redemption. Hence, the Church from the day of Pentecost has been most zealous in defending her honor and her purity, praising her for giving a Savior to the world. All benefits, all graces, all heavenly favors come from Christ and descend into the Body of the Church through Mary.

When the wine of your life is failing and your faith is weak, when your charity is growing cold, go to her who at Cana's feast interceded to her Divine Son for the replenishing of the wine of gladness. When your whole frame racks beneath the tempter, fly to the patronage of her Immaculate Heart, whose heel crushes the head of the serpent. When the cold hand of death is laid upon those whom you love, and your heart seems torn in two, climb to the Hill of Calvary to be consoled by the Mother of Sorrows who is also a source of our joy.

When sin corrodes your soul and rusts your heart and you are weary without God, then have recourse to Mary the Refuge of Sinners, for she, the Sinless One, knows what sin is—she, too, lost her God. When the sweet inspirations of the Holy Spirit call you away from the passing tin and tinsel of earthly joys to the life of sanctity, then pray to her that you may follow her dictates to love her Divine Son: "Whatsoever he shall say to you, do."

Never was it known that anyone who fled to her protection, or asked her help, was left unaided. She is our advocate before the Father. Until eternity dawns, you who live in the hope of that eternal union with the daughter of the Father, the mother of the Son, and the spouse of the Holy Spirit, pray from the bottom of your hearts that prayer which is the counterpart of the Lord's Prayer, the prayer of the children of Mary, and say to her:

Hail Mary, full of grace, the Lord is with thee.
Blessed art thou amongst women,
and blessed is the fruit of thy womb, Jesus.
Holy Mary, Mother of God, pray for us sinners,
now and at the hour of our death. Amen.

Eighteen

Alive in Christ

WHATEVER WE MAY SAY of the world and its wickedness, there is nevertheless hidden in the heart of it the beautiful instinct to remember those who died in sacrifice. Every nation under the sun has its memorial day consecrated to the blessed memory of the heroes of its battles and its wars. Now, if there be such a remembered gratitude for those who died for a nation, why wouldn't there be a memorial for him who died for the world? If we remember those who sacrificed themselves for others, why shouldn't we remember him from whose death all sacrifice has received its sacred seal and noble inspiration? Calvary is too beautiful to be lost! The Cross bearing the burden of the Savior of all is too holy to be forgotten! "Greater love than this no man has, than he lay down his life for his friends." Such love deserves to be perpetuated. Lest anyone forget—and how quickly they do— our Lord resolved to institute a memorial of his sacrifice. Most people at the approach of death prepare their last wills and testaments, in which they dispose of their properties, their titles, their wealth. On the eve of his death our Lord made his last will and testament but, unlike humans, he left that which no one on dying ever left: namely, himself.

This he could do, being God. He would leave himself not in any indifferent act of his life, but in that supreme act where love reached its peak in the sacrifice of Good Friday. The particular means he chose to represent the awful separation of his blood from his body on the Cross were under the symbols of bread and wine. Gathering his apostles about him in the Upper Room on the night that has since been called Holy Thursday, he anticipated the sacrifice of the Cross which would follow in less than eighteen hours.

By the separate consecration of first the bread and then the wine, he symbolically represented his future crucifixion in which his body as the Bread of Heaven, and his blood as the Wine of Life, were to be separated one from the other for the redemption of the world. He was thus offering up what was in store for him; anticipating, as it were, his Baptism of Blood by pledging himself to death in the sight of his Father and the human race. Everyone knows the circumstances of that evening. He took bread in his hand "and blessed and broke: and gave to his disciples, and said, 'Take and eat. This is my body.' And taking the chalice, he gave thanks, and gave to them, saying, 'Drink you all of this. For this is my body and the new testament, which shall be shed for many unto remission of sins.'"

Then looking forward to all ages and all times, and to all hearts who would ever crave a memorial of the death that gave us everlasting life, he said, "Do this is in remembrance of me."

On the next afternoon at three o'clock that which he anticipated and foreshadowed and mystically represented in the Last Supper came to pass: his body was delivered to executioners, his blood was poured forth.

Now, here we are, [two thousand] years removed from that Last Supper and that crimsoned Golgotha. Keeping both in mind, and the fact that he the God-man begged us to remember his last will and testament, cast your eyes about the world and ask yourself these questions:

- Who have done that which he asked us to do the night of the Last Supper in commemoration of him?

- Who have taken bread and wine into their hands and by the mystical sword of the words of consecration symbolically represented the separation of both on a cross, where love sank to the depths and arose as sacrifice?
- Who have a daily memorial ceremony in which there is reenacted, in an unbloody manner, the tragedy of Calvary?

For the answer enter into any Catholic Church in the world and during the early morning hours you will see a priest, whose heritage is one with those of the Upper Room, mount an altar, take bread and wine in his hands, breathe over them the very words of our Lord himself, and as a bell tinkles and all heads in church bow in prayer, you will see the priest kneel in adoration of the Bread which is the Body and the Wine which is the Blood of our Lord and Savior. And as both are lifted above his head, as the Cross was lifted above the earth, you will understand how that same Lord erects Calvary once again amidst hearts that love and hands that crucify.

Someone has remembered his words. "Do this in remembrance of me" has not fallen on deaf ears. Calvary was too beautiful to be forgotten. It is remembered! It is commemorated! It is reenacted! It is re-presented! It is prolonged through space and time—and its memorial is the Mass.

There is grave danger that we might believe the Mass to be only a memorial ceremony, such as that which we have on Memorial Day for our hero soldiers; or as a kind of imitation of the Last Supper on the stage of the altar in which we are passive spectators; or as a prayer in which there is only a repetition of the beautiful words of the Last Supper. No! The Mass is none of these things. *The Mass is the sacrifice of the Mystical Body of Christ, and is one with Calvary, which was the sacrifice of the physical body of Christ.*

The Mass, in other words, is a supra-temporal reality,

by which the glorified Christ in heaven prolongs his sacrifice on the Cross by and through us. Though he is priest and victim, the manner of offering is not the same in both the Mass and the Cross. On the Cross he was alone; in the Mass he is with us. On the Cross he offered up his life for all who would one day be incorporated to his Mystical Body; in the Mass he renews the sacrifice for all who are actually incorporated into that Mystical Body. On the Cross the historical Christ offered himself; in the Mass the Mystical Christ (which is Christ *and* us) offers himself. The Cross was in Jerusalem as a space, and it was [two thousand] years ago in time; the Mass is the same Cross made actual throughout space and time. There is no time or space between Calvary and Now. On the Cross the human nature of Christ was susceptible to suffering; in the Mass his human nature is glorified, and hence he cannot suffer, except through other human natures that make up his Mystical Body. The Cross purchases redemption; the Mass applies it. The Mass is the tremendous experience of the reality of Golgotha with its forgiveness and its love, its power and its pardon, extended and prolonged even unto this hour.

The Mass, I say, is the sacrifice of the Mystical Body, the Church, and not a mere empty symbolism of Calvary. On the Cross, Our Lord took the human nature which he assumed from his mother in the unity of his Person and, as Priest on the Cross, offered it to his Father in reparation for the sins of humanity. That human nature after the Resurrection and Ascension was elevated to the glory of heaven. The human nature of Jesus can therefore never suffer again. It has entered into its reward beyond all crucifixions and deaths. "Christ rising again from the dead, dies now no more; death shall no more have dominion over him." *He can therefore add nothing to his priestly office except by and through us.* And it is this he has chosen to do. He wills to do with other human natures scattered throughout the world what he did with his own human nature taken from his Virgin Mother. He, therefore, as Head of the Mystical Body in heaven, calls others to himself—other Peters, Pauls, Johns, Marthas, Marys, Teresas, Augustines, Cyrils, Boscos, Little Flowers— in a word, all the millions of baptized men and women who have been incorporated to him by baptism—as his new Mystical Body. He asks them to give him their human natures in love, that he may continue his redemptive priesthood by and through them, so that not only he in his own human nature, but *he in ours*, may offer them anew to his heavenly Father in an unending act of priestly sacrifice.

As a great patriot in time of national crisis seeks not only to offer his own life for the sake of his country, but also strives to rally others to himself that, through their corporate selflessness, the whole nation may be preserved, so he, the glorified Christ in heaven, seeks the enlistment of you and me—all of us—under his headship, that we may offer ourselves *with* his offering on the Cross, to win the triumphs of other loving Calvaries, even as he did.

This enlistment takes place at the offertory of the Mass, where we are present under the form of bread and wine. Just as bread is one, though it is made from a multiplicity of grains of wheat; just as wine is one, though made from a multiplicity of grapes, so we are one in Christ, though a multiplicity of cells in the Mystical Body. Furthermore, bread and wine represent the substantial nourishment of life. The grain of wheat which is the fat of the land, and the grape which is the marrow and blood of the earth, are fundamental means of renewing our substance and refreshing our blood. When, therefore, people bring bread and wine to the altar, they are equivalently bringing themselves.

If there is anything that adequately describes the part of the faithful in the offertory of the Mass, it is the picture of our Lord standing on the hill of Calvary before his great Cross.

Crowded about him on the same hill we stand with our little crosses stretched on the ground alongside his great model Cross. The very moment he makes the offertory of his life, and walks to his Cross to prove that his love for us is stronger than death, we walk to our little crosses, make the offertory of our lives in union with him, to prove that our love of Righteousness, Justice, Truth, Love, and God is stronger than our love of that life which quickly passes away. As the Offertory of the Mass is the *offering* of Christ and us, so the Consecration of the Mass is the *sacrifice* of Christ and us. The Vine sacrificed himself on the Cross; the Vine and the Branches now sacrifice themselves in the Mass. The primary meaning of the words of consecration, then, refers to the Vine: This is the Body and this is the Blood of Christ, renewing the sacrifice of Calvary. But the secondary meaning refers to the branches united to the Vine to form the Mystical Body, in which you and I, all members of the Church, say:

This is my body, this is my blood. I offered myself with You at the Offertory; now I immolate myself with You at the Consecration. Take my body and my blood with You to the Cross; take my body and blood with all the pains, sorrows, agonies; with their capacities for love, for service, and for repentance; take them with You to the Cross, that they may be united with your sacrifice which alone makes them acceptable to your heavenly Father; that they may purchase me to yourself in *act,* as You did purchase me in *hope* at Calvary. Take not merely my possessions, my titles, my apostolate, my zeal, my energy, but take all that I am, the very substance of my life: my body, my blood. Take them, make them one with your sacrifice as the drop of water becomes one with the wine. Possess them so that what is mine is yours, so that the heavenly Father in looking down upon your renewed Calvary may find that there is but one Body and one Blood, which is yours, his beloved Son, in whom the Father is well pleased.

The Mass, then, is *Calvary recalled, renewed,* and *applied*—the only thing in this world which makes it possible for us to follow his command, "Take up your cross daily and follow me." In no other act of his Mystical Life does he come so close to us. Bethlehem is with us in the Real Presence; Christ's voice is with us in the Church; his hands are with us in the sacraments. But his love unto death is with us in the continued Sacrifice of the Mass.

Nineteen

Two Broken Hearts

WE KNOW VERY WELL there is no other name under heaven by which we may be saved than "Christ": that it is only by the shedding of the blood of Christ that our sins are forgiven, and that Christ has died but once. We can go way back to the Old Testament for a confirmation of this.

When the Israelites left Egypt they were short of water—at the very beginning of their journey. And God said to Moses, "Take your rod and strike that rock." (Then the Scripture says the rock was Christ.) "Strike that rock and water will flow from it." That, incidentally, is the symbol of the Church: the permanence of the rock, with the mobility of the waters. So the people had an abundance to drink. Thirty-eight years later there was another shortage of water. God said to Moses, "Speak to the rock." And Moses turned to his people and said, "You stiff-necked people. Don't you think I can draw water from this rock?" And he struck the rock, and water came forth. But God said, "For that, you will not go to the Promised Land. Three times Moses begged, but could not get close; he could only see the land from afar, but could never enter it. Why was he denied entrance? Because the rock was Christ, and Christ is to be struck but once: on Calvary. There's no other salvation but in Christ. From that point on, we intercede to Christ. We speak to Him. Moses, through that symbolism, had implied that there was still another striking for salvation.

The same thing happened to the sons of Aaron. These two priests were just ordained. And they came into the tabernacle, where there was the altar of sacrifice, the altar of incense beyond the golden candlestick, the bread of perpetual presence, and the two sons lit the fires of the altar of intercession. But it was a strange fire (says the Scripture), for which they were struck dead by God. And Aaron did not move. He knew the justice of God's judgment; and Moses said, "Remove the bodies." Then they went on with the liturgy. Why were these newly ordained priests struck dead? Because the fires of the altar of intercession must be lighted from the altar of sacrifice. There is no intercession except through sacrifice. They skipped Calvary, as it were, and thought that heaven would be open and they could have intercession to God without a sacrifice. See how strict and severe God is in driving home this truth to us about the death and sacrifice of Christ.

Now we come to the continuation of this striking. When the Blessed Mother brought her Babe to Simeon, he spoke words that wounded her heart: "A sword will pierce your heart." And from that moment on, the Blessed Mother was waiting for the striking of the Rock. A new sword of Damocles swung over her head. About the fourth century before Christ, the king of Syracuse was a certain Dionysius, and he was very often praised by a certain Damocles. One night the king gave a banquet for Damocles, who found that immediately suspended above his chair was a sharp sword that hung only by a hair. The king wanted him to know how perilous and uneasy was his own life that at any moment it could be taken. And so we have a new Christian sword of Damocles, and it is unsheathed by the old man Simeon who speaks to Mary, so that Mary lives always under the shadow of this sword. When will it fall? She must have thought of it particularly when Herod unsheathed his swords. Why did he do it? Can you imagine, for example, Germany, the moment

Hitler was born, killing all male children under two years of age to prevent Hitler? Or the people of Georgia doing that when Stalin was two years old? They could not have known what would happen to Stalin or to Hitler. But Herod tried to take his life. Why? Because Herod knew the prophecy that the line of Herod would end with the coming of our Blessed Lord. And it did—with Herod the Great's own son.

Mary thought that maybe the sword would fall then, and then all during his life, particularly when he began his public life. Şaint Luke describes in his gospel that long journey from Galilee up to Jerusalem. He is walking into his death, and as he comes into Jerusalem there's a warrant out for his arrest. He stays that night in the adjoining village of Bethany with friends. And the next day, in the face of this warrant, and the police who were sent to arrest him, he makes a triumphant entry. And Mary must have wondered, since he had opposed these—not the law, but religion—that maybe they would not draw a sword against him. She must have been worried, too, about Judas. That name "Iscariot" bothered her. Some say that "Iscariot" comes from *secarius*, "the dagger-bearer." As an extreme nationalist, he was against the Romans. Would he—now that he had defected from our Lord at the time of the announcement of the Eucharist—would he use it against the Savior? And then the night our Blessed Lord went into the Garden, Peter had two swords. One of them he swung wildly, hacking off the ear of the servant of the high priest. Then there was a flash of swords. Mary must have heard about that and wondered if that sword above her head was going to fall on her Son and on her. And even her Divine Son said to them who came to arrest him, "You have come out with sticks and staffs and swords to arrest me. I have done nothing that is hidden. I have spoken openly to you." Mary waited for that sword, but it did not fall.

And finally, he comes to his Cross. There we see Mary, John, and Mary Magdalene. The Blessed Mother standing, because she was sharing in redemption, as much as the new Eve could share. Our Lord had spoken to her and announced that she was the new Eve, but John was the firstborn of the Church. And Mary would have the moon, which is the Church, under her feet. Our Blessed Lord now comes to the end of his earthly life. The prodigal Son is finally going back home. He had wasted his substance, his precious body and blood. And now, penniless, he goes back again to the Father's house. And just as some comets, only after a long period of time, complete their orbit and then come back to the starting point, as if to salute him who sent them on their way, so now he prepares to return again to his starting point. He always said, "No one takes my life away from me. I lay it down of myself." So the last word is spoken "in a loud voice," says Scripture, even though he is draining himself of his blood. Magdalene can feel it on her hair. Mary kisses it as it touches her hand. John caresses the Cross. And then finally there is a breathing. He *breathes* out the Spirit. The Greek word in the gospel suggests that he "transmitted" it. Here he is transmitting his Spirit to Mary, the symbol of the Church, and to John, the beginning of the Church, who stands for all of us, the disciples who love our Blessed Lord. See how, before Pentecost, there was this giving of the Spirit, not only to those beneath the Cross, but to the apostles and, finally, to the Body which is the Church. So he transmits his Spirit. There is a rupture of the heart, to a rapture of love, as he commends himself into the hands of his heavenly Father. "Into thy hands I commend my spirit." What a relief to be away from the hands of man! At last, back in the Father's hands.

Now we must picture two scenes, Jerusalem and Calvary, and two veils. This is the Day of Atonement. Hundreds of thousands of sheep shedding their blood, symbolic of the Lamb of God who is to come, and who has already come. And the high priest is now about to perform that ritual that happens only once a year. He puts on his miter, with the words "Holy, Holy, Holy" written on it, and bells that are attached to the miter, so that when he enters beyond that veil the whole congregation will know he is there. And this veil, and this temple of Jerusalem, which was being built then by Herod, was about sixty feet high—purple, blue, and scarlet—and at the side were two white cherubim. They must have worried Mary, because she remembered Eden. When the first parents fell God stationed cherubim with a flaming sword that moved this way and that way in order to indicate that no one will ever get back again into that garden unless he's pierced with that sword. Mary knew this and thought about it every time she looked at it. And she thought, too, of that prophecy of Zechariah, who said, "The Lord of Hosts speaks. Strike my shepherd." So this symbolic veil that now hangs before the temple is about to be entered by the high priest. Since it happens only once a year, it's the great liturgical ceremony of all Israel.

But there's another veil: It is the veil of the flesh of Christ. Saint John, in describing the Incarnation, writes that he tabernacled himself, he tented himself, among us. He tabernacled himself through the flesh. Divinity was inside of that flesh. And that flesh is called in Scripture "the veil." So we have two veils: the great veil in the temple with the cherubim, and this veil of the Savior who has just spent his life for us. And now comes the sword. Mary was waiting for it to fall, and she sees the centurion come with a lance. The bones of the two thieves have been broken, because the two thieves were not yet dead. And the Jews would not permit a dead body to hang on the cross on the eve of their Sabbath. So the bones of the thieves were crushed and smashed. But not a bone of the Lord's body was ever struck, in fulfillment of the prophecy. The soldier takes this lance, comes beneath the Cross of Christ, and plunges it into the side of Christ. John even quotes Zechariah. John said, "Lord of Hosts,...

strike my shepherd." The man in the Roman army fulfills the prophecy. But just at the moment when the veil of this flesh is being rent, lo and behold, as the high priest in Jerusalem takes the blood of the lamb and sprinkles it upon that veil, which was the condition of his entering, suddenly this great curtain is rent from top to bottom. Not from bottom to top, for a man could do that, but from top to bottom, and collapses. And that Holy of Holies which could be seen but once a year, and then only to the high priest, is revealed to all. But at that same moment, when the centurion struck the heart of Christ, piercing the veil of his flesh, *heaven was opened*! The Holy of Holies was revealed!

Everyone who wills can enter the sanctuary of God. As the Epistle to the Hebrews puts it, in 10:19–20, "So my friends, the blood of Jesus makes us free to enter boldly into the sanctuary. By the new and living way, which he has opened for us through the veil of his flesh."

The sanctuary is open. And the Lord asked of us only one thing: to watch an hour, to join in the combat against evil. The heart of Christ is now manifested to the world in a new way. But we have noticed that as time has gone on, we've had many revelations. The latest revelations have been about the Sacred Heart and the Immaculate Heart.

The heart is the last thing we give. We have friends whom we love, we give gifts, communications, treats; but the heart—that's the last thing we can give, because it's the last and final testimony of our love. And as the world grows old, the Lord says to us, "I want to show you my Heart again." Through Saint Margaret Mary, the Sacred Heart reveals, *I have loved humanity to the fullest. And oh, how often people have shown me coldness, indifference, disrespect, and neglect in the sacrament of my love.*

The Blessed Mother gave her Heart, too. And when she gave her Heart, she said to the children, "Let us pray. Pray to the Sacred Heart to make up for all the sacrileges that are committed against the Lord in the Blessed Sacrament." These two revelations prove to us that the Heart of Christ in the Eucharist gives us the energy to combat evil, and someday we're going to see this Heart.

Saint John, who stood at the Cross, and who understood the Heart of Christ better than anyone else because he leaned against it on the night of the Last Supper, said, "All shall look on him whom they have pierced." And then, at the end of his life when he began to write the Book of Revelation, at the very beginning of it he describes Christ coming again. "Behold, he is coming with the clouds. Every eye shall see him. And among them, those who pierced him, and all the peoples of the world shall lament in remorse." We shall all see the heart of the Lord. Because for that heart we have been pleading. And as we renew that love we search for that centurion. Where is he? Centurion, come back! You've already acknowledged that he is the Son of God. But come back! Come back, even though his blood is at the end of your lance. Come back, even though that sword fell, and with one blow pierced two hearts—physically the Heart of Christ and mystically the Heart of Mary. One spear, and two broken hearts, for the world of broken bread. So, centurion, come back. We want to tell you that there's another way to get closer to the Heart of Christ than wounding him.

We know what that way is: the daily holy hour. I invite you to meet me at that Heart for one hour today, tomorrow, the day after tomorrow, and every day as God gives us days, until we all meet—and we will, each and every one of us— in the Heart of Christ through the intercession of the Heart of Mary.

Glory be to God!

Twenty

Complain!

God does not frown on your complaint.
Did not His Mother in the Temple ask:
"Son! Why hast thou done so to us?"
And did not Christ on the Cross complain:
"My God! Why hast Thou abandoned Me?"
If the Son asked the Father,
And the Mother the Son—"Why?"
Why should not you?

But let your wails be to God,
And not to man,
Asking not, "Why does God do this to me?"
But: "Why, O God, dost Thou treat me so?"
Talk not *about* God, as Satan did to Eve:
"Why did God command you?"
But talk *to* God as Christ to His Father.

And at the end of your sweet complaining prayer
You will say: "Father, into Thy Hands I commend my
spirit."
You will not so much be taken down
As the thief on the left,
But be taken up as the thief
Who heard: "This day, Paradise."

They who complain to others never see God's purposes
They who complain to God find that
Their Passion, like Christ's, turns into compassion.

Only He who made your wound can heal it.
The Love that tightened your bow-strings
Did so, not in hurt, but in love of music.

Do not all lovers ask in doubt: "Do you love me?"
Ask that of the Tremendous Lover
And each scar will seem a kiss!

God is not "way up there."
He is taking another body—your own
To carry on the world's redemption.

Too few offer Him a human nature
Like Mary at the angel's call—
So He conscripts you, drafts you,
Inducts you into His Army.

Complain that your shoulders
Ache beneath your pack—
But see His own smarting
Under a cross beam.

Complaint to God is dialogue,
And dialogue is prayer.
Not the ready-made, packaged, memorized
Lip-service of the book and candle,
but the encounter and the union
That only lovers know!

Twenty-One

Reparation

UNITED AS WE ARE to one another in the Mystical Body of Christ, there is reciprocity, mutual sympathy, and a sense of cooperativeness between and among us. We should therefore feel responsible toward one another as the various parts of the human body feel responsible toward one another. "As the eye cannot say to the hand, 'I do not need your help'; nor again the head to the feet, 'I have no need of you'"; so neither can we dispense ourselves from other members of the Mystical Body, regardless of how lowly their position, or regardless of how different their vocation.

Now of the various sympathies existing between us as members of the Mystical Body, I wish to mention three: sorrow, joy, and reparation.

First, there is sorrow: If I hurt my hand, my whole body feels the pain—for my hand is one with my body. If my eye sees a blow about to be directed against the ear, the eye does not say, "It is not going to strike me, and therefore I need not worry." As a matter of fact, the eye does seek to prevent injury to the ear, for both are one because they are parts of the same organism. Now in the Mystical Body of Christ, the sorrow, the suffering, and the persecution of the Church in one part of the world should be felt by the Church in all parts of the world. On this logic the Church in Mexico, for example, is part of the Mystical Body as much as the arm is part of the human body. What it suffers, therefore, the whole

Church should feel as its own. As Saint Paul has said, "If one member suffer anything, all the members suffer with it."

Now do we actually feel the sufferings of the Church in Mexico, or in Germany, or any country, as we should? Do we realize that we are one with them, because we are parts of the same body vivified by the same Spirit? Do we pray for them? Do we feel sad at the loss of that faith by those who once possessed it? Do we grieve for those who once loved God and then left the paths of peace? Do we who have some of the world's goods realize that the poor parts of this, our Body, have need of our superfluities? Do national boundaries blind our vision to that wider outlook where there is only that supranationalism in Christ?

When the Church is being persecuted in one part of the world, when churches are pillaged, bishops exiled, the faithful martyred, do we feel that their pain and their sorrow is ours, as much as the pain in the arm is the pain in the whole body? If we are insensitive to these sorrows of the Church in other parts of the world, then we are insensitive to our membership in the Mystical Body of Christ. Then we are calloused to those finer sympathies which prove not only that we are gentlemen but, what is more refined, Christians worthy of the name. The interaction of the moon on the tides, the sympathy between a baby's cry and the vibration of a distant star, is as nought compared to that finer interaction and sympathy between Christian and Christian in the Body of Christ which is his Church.

What is true of sorrow and pain in the Mystical Body is true also of its joy. In the human body, if the tongue tastes something sweet the whole body rejoices. In like manner in the Church, Saint Paul tell us, "If one member glory, all the members rejoice with it." When, therefore, the Church canonizes a saint, when there is an increase of communions in the Church, when sinners return to the faith and do penance which makes even the angels rejoice, when the spirit of prayer and contemplation grows in the souls of men and women as worldliness decreases, when foreign missionaries make new conquests for Christ—each of these should make us rejoice, for it is a joy of a part of our body.

If we rejoice, then, we are conscious of our solidarity in the Mystical Body of Christ; then we are prepared to understand not merely the *sympathy* we must have for the joys and sorrows of others, but also the *reparation* we should offer for those members who stand in need of it.

The analogy of the human body makes clear this idea of reparation. It is a well-established fact that all the cells and nerves and organs of the body have their keyboard in the brain. The connection between the right hand and the left is not direct, but mediate, that is, it is established through the central nervous system. In the event of perfectly established and harmonious relations between the center and its members, there is a perfect unanimity and reciprocity between the members themselves, which guarantees mutual help and assistance. For example, let a speck of dust enter the eye and at once the hand flies up to minister. Let a person slip in the street and sprain his foot and the other foot will do double duty all the way home. If a person burned his face, doctors would graft skin from another part of his body and apply it to his face; if a person is suffering from anemia, doctors will transfuse blood from another member of society to that weak individual, to cure him of that anemic condition. This fine fellowship and fealty spring out of perfectly sustained relations with the head.

Now in the Mystical Body all members who are one by obedience to the same visible head can therefore be of service one to the other. If it is possible for the hand to help the eye, do you not think it possible for a Catholic in America to help a Catholic in India, because both are connected through the keyboard of the Vicar of Christ? If it is possible to graft skin, is it not also possible to graft prayer? If it is possible to transfuse blood, is it not also possible to transfuse sacrifice? This process of atoning and sacrificing ourselves for other members of the Mystical Body is what is known as reparation. Such is the meaning of Saint Paul's words: "Bear you one another's burdens; so you also shall fulfill the law of Christ." Such, too, is the reason for the cloistered communities in the Church, such as the Carmelites and Poor Clares, the Trappists and Chartreuse, and many others whose supreme business in life it is to repair the harm done by others, and to bring succor to those who cannot help themselves.

The world is full of those who sin and atone not; who offend God and never repent; who have their sins forgiven, but who never do penance. These poor, burnt, anemic, wounded members of the Mystical Body of Christ may yet be saved by those who out of their superfluities expend spiritual wealth for the salvation of souls. The world which asks of such saintly mortified souls hidden away in cloisters and convents, "What good do they do?" fails to understand that in the order of divine life they are doing for the wounded on the spiritual battlefields of the Church that which, in the order of human life, nurses and doctors are doing on the battlefields of the world. And since the saving of a soul is immeasurably more important than the saving of a body, we may very well ask if the comparison is justified at all.

In these days when the world regards a sin as a lesser evil than a headache, the value of reparation in the Mystical Body is apt to be overlooked. It needs to be repeated that reparation exists because there is sin. In every sin there is a double element: the joy of a forbidden fruit and the act of disobedience against God. Equilibrium can be established between the two, therefore, only by a commensurate pain to atone for the forbidden joy, and a compensating repentance to atone for the act of disobedience. Of these two elements the latter is more important, for it gives to the first its moral significance. Otherwise pain would be pain for the sake of pain, and not sacrifice. Then we would be like the Hindu mystics who glorify suffering as an end in itself. It is the sorrow, the contrition, and the desire to love God which changes pain into sacrifice—for what is pain but sacrifice without love?

But it is not enough to be sorry for our sins. Sin involves a debt, and the debt must be paid. It is not sufficient for a person who has run into great debt to say to his creditors, "I am very sorry I have contracted such debts. I will not run up any more in the future." He must *pay the debts,* in addition to being contrite. So likewise with sin. It is not enough to tell God we are sorry for our sins; we must pay the debts contracted by them—and if there was fun in running them up, there must be pain in tracking them down. If we take a hundred steps in the wrong direction, we must put our foot down one hundred times to get back in the right direction. Where there was forbidden joy, there must be willing sacrifice. If we sow cockle in joy with our wheat, we must pluck it out in pain. There is no pardon without reparation. That is why beneath all the liturgical difference of all peoples, there has always been sacrifice. They have testified with Paul that "without shedding of blood there is no remission."

Thus it is by reparation for others that we "fill up those things that are wanting of the sufferings of Christ, in my flesh, for his Body which is the Church." This means that the redemption of the physical body of Christ is complete, but not the redemption of his Mystical Body.

The Cross, then, is the focal point of all creation. Creation was only a prelude to the drama of Calvary. Creation exists for no other reason than to have a cross erected upon it. And the inspiration of the Sacrifice of the Cross was love wherein God who loves humankind poured out the crushed-out sweetness of his Sacred Heart. Love is the reason for all reparation, for love by its nature means not to have, to own, to possess, but to *be* had, to *be* owned, to *be* possessed.

That is why love always expresses itself in terms of arrows and darts—something that wounds. Its greatest luxury is to spend; its greatest joy is to serve; its keenest pleasure is to throw itself on the altar of sacrifice for the one loved. That is why Saint Augustine could exclaim, "Give me a heart that has really loved, and I will tell him what God is." Every human heart that has ever been in love, or has ever risen one step above the modern wallowing in sex, knows this. And yet these revealing moments, when your heart stands naked before you and you see its authentic fires, are but poor and partial reflections of the great Sun of Love which is God. There is not a mother in the world whose white passion of love swings open the great portals of flesh to bring into the world the self-gift of a child; there is not a father in the world who has thought his highest heaven on earth to bear a cross for that child; there is not a saint on earth whose passionless passion for souls has not, like a pelican, wounded itself to nourish with its merits the fledglings of Christ's flock.

In a word, there has never been a heart that ever beat once in sacrificing love which did not understand that, since God is love, he should fittingly overflow the boundaries of heaven, and from the Cross reach into a wounded side to give us the hostage of his Sacred Heart.

Twenty-Two

The World's Greatest Need

THERE IS A FAMINE abroad on the earth—a famine not of bread, for we have had too much of that, and our luxury has made us forget God; a famine not of gold, for the glitter of so much of it has blinded us to the meaning of the twinkle of the stars, but a famine of a more serious kind, one that threatens nearly every country in the world: the famine of really great men and women.

There is little in the lives of human beings that is heroic, little that is genuinely self-sacrificing, little that is high. In the field of politics there are but few who follow principles rather than public opinion. The great majority of those in political life, instead of leading the masses by noble directions, follow them into ignoble ways. The age is too timid for individuality, too calculating for enthusiasm, too weak for heroism; and what is true in the political order is true in the religious.

Religion walks in silver slippers. Its modern prophets cannot cut against the grain of long prejudices. They are jealously favorable to modern views, whether they be true or not, just because they are modern. Our prophets avoid taking sides when truth is concerned, for fear they make enemies. They spread their sails to every wave of popularity and would not dare to say a word against a dominant prejudice or a triumphant error. They enjoy the beatitude that Christ never promised, and they enjoy it because they are weak. It is not our institutions that are failing us today; it is our people. We need great men and women!

This statement about our civilizations suffering from the nemesis of mediocrity may be challenged by an appeal to the so-called great people of our day, for example, those of great wealth who have started with nothing and have amassed fortunes; those who have succeeded in great feats of engineering, of tunneling under rivers like moles, or spanning continents on wings of steel. This is a type of greatness, I will admit, but it is a greatness that is external to the person himself. Greatness is not in muscles, in gold, nor in educational institutions, nor in anything that strikes the eye. It consists in something that requires almost a new sense of appreciation. Greatness is not something external to a person, but rather it is something internal. Greatness is a quality of the heart and mind and soul by which a person conquers not so much the tides of the sea as the tides of his passion. Greatness consists in a fine sense of justice, righteousness, and charity; and judged by this standard it is true that we are equipped like gods to rule over nature, but to rule over ourselves we are equipped like pygmies. Yet it is in this self-conquest that true greatness consists.

The world's greatest need, then, is someone who will understand that there is no greater conquest than victory over oneself; someone who will realize that real worth is achieved not so much by activity as by silence; who will seek first the Kingdom of God and his justice, and put into actual practice the law that it is only by dying to the life of the body that we ever live to the life of the Spirit; who will brave the taunts of a Good Friday to win the joy of an Easter Sunday; who will, like a lightning flash, burn away the bonds of feeble interest which tie down our energies to the world; who with a fearless voice, like John the Baptist, will arouse our enfeebled nature out of the sleek dream of unheroic repose; someone who will gain victories not by stepping down from the Cross and compromising with the world, but who will suffer in order to conquer the world. In a word, what we need are saints, for saints are truly great souls.

Just suppose that we could turn loose in America at this time twelve saints. Let us assume that none of them were university trained, but that all their knowledge came from prayer; that they were not rich, but poor, like Saint Francis of Assisi; that they had all their beauty in their souls and not on their faces, like Saint Vincent de Paul; that none of them were practical as the world counts practicality, but all of them impractical in the sense that but one-fourth of their waking time would be spent in activity, and the rest in prayer.

Suppose that these individuals who had an invisible consecration laid upon them, who had the zeal of Christ burning in their hearts, tore away the accumulated cobweb of our sophistry, confounded our conventional morality with sincerity, let the stroke of their challenge ring on the broad shield of the world's hypocrisies, paid no respect to slogans, preached the lesson of justice on street corners, and repeated at each available moment that it is only by being conformed to the passion of Christ that we can ever be conformed to the glory of his risen body!

What would follow if they went into the world? A roar of execration! They would please no one. Belonging to no party, all parties would oppose them. Rich men would deride them. Learned men would ignore them. Modern Pharisees would lay snares for them, and call them politically dangerous. They would be called fools, fanatics, devils, mad. People would say that they were actuated by mawkish sentimentality; that their zeal was just a pretense; that they were mystics; that only the ignorant would follow them. They would have more stones thrown at them than others have flowers. But these twelve, these great ones, would effect a greater spirituality in America than all the combined humanitarian agencies counting tens of thousands of members.

They would elevate more hearts and souls to the love of God; they would purge out more wickedness in a day than reformed societies would do in a lifetime, simply because they were great with the greatness of Christ.

Now we all cannot become saints as these twelve that I have pictured, but we can all become saints to a certain degree, and I am going to try to explain in simple psychological terms how saints are made. I assume without further ado that the grace of God is the one thing necessary, and that God will give that grace to those who do his will. I am concerned merely with the natural elements of sanctity, or the psychological steps that lead to the state of sainthood, and these are three: a sense of emptiness, a knowledge, and an exchange.

First of all, I say that they are made by an experience of the emptiness of the world, and its absolute incapacity to give peace and happiness to the human heart. Consult your own experience. When you were children you looked forward to Christmas Day, and in anticipation you imagined all the joys that would be yours with the possession of your toys, the sight of the lighted tree, and the unlimited taste of fruits and candies. When finally Christmas Day did come, and you had played with the toys (and it was not long until you were "played out") and had tasted the sweetmeats and blown out the last candle on the tree, you then crept into your bed and said in your own little heart of hearts that, somehow or other, it did not come up to your expectations. It did not, because nothing does.

That experience of childhood has been repeated a thousand times since. Individuals look forward to the possession of power, they finally get it, and still they are unhappy. People crave wealth, they have a hundred times more than they need, and still they want more, and their wanting it makes them unhappy. Even the loss of the least of it robs them of joy, as the plucking of a single hair from a head that is full of it gives pain. Nothing ever comes up to our expectations.

Well, why is this? The reason is that in looking forward to the things of this world, we use our imagination, which, as a faculty of the soul, is spiritual and therefore capable of imagining infinite things. I can imagine, for example, a mountain of gold, but I have never seen one. I can imagine a castle on the Hudson River that has a thousand rooms, and each wall blazing with diamonds and emeralds, but I have never seen that castle, and perhaps never will.

Now the pleasure of the future, the joys that I hope to obtain, the power that I desire to wield, the wealth that I desire to possess—all of these, as long as they are not actually in my possession, become endowed with the infinity that belongs to the imagination. In a certain sense they become spiritualized and idealized, and hence take on something of the blessedness and infinity of imagination. But when finally these imaginations or expectations are realized, they are material, they are local, definite, concrete, finite, cribbed, confined. In the mind they were ideal, and hence almost unbounded; in reality, they are concrete, and therefore very limited. Hence there arises a tremendous disparity between the infinite imagination I had of these things, and their finite realization. When the things actually do come, they come with a sense of loss. We feel that in their becoming actual or real, they lost something of the beauty with which we had imaginatively endowed them. A sense of emptiness or void then comes over the soul. We feel that we have been cheated out of something, for the realization compared to our imagination is like trying to fill a valley with a pebble; a terrible sense of emptiness creeps over the soul, and this sense of void is really a call of God. In very simple terms, it means that we cannot expect happiness here below. It also means we are made for an infinite happiness, otherwise we never could have imagined it. And it further means that we can never obtain it here below, for otherwise we would never have this terrible feeling of loss, disappointment, and emptiness.

Two escapes are possible from this feeling of emptiness and dissatisfaction of the world, or better still, from the voice of God. One is to drown the call of God by seeking new pleasures, new stimuli, new excitements. Some souls use the remedy and go on chasing butterflies and golden pots at the end of the rainbow. They throw themselves into pleasures that satisfy a very small part of themselves, but never their whole being. Others let loose the reins of duty upon the flanks of the steeds of passion, and gallop down the avenues of pleasures, always being made more hungry by that which satisfies, until at last despair drives them to suicide and double death.

Saintly souls, on the other hand, when they feel this sense of uneasiness in their souls, conclude that happiness is not to be found on this earth; that they were made for God, and that their only unhappiness comes from a failure to tend toward him. At this point begins the second stage in the development of great ones, namely, a knowledge (and by knowledge I mean an understanding) of our Lord and Savior.

Let me here again appeal to your personal experience. You may have heard a great deal about a certain person, about his mannerisms, about his severity, about his rigorous life. You know only *about* him, but you do not *know* him. With this meager knowledge you frankly avow that you do not care for him. But after spending five minutes in his company, your whole feeling has completely changed. Knowledge changed your whole outlook on him and converted hate into the beginning of love. In much the same way that the prejudice of Nathaniel against our Blessed Lord was changed by just two sentences from our Lord's lips, sentences that swept away prejudice, so it is with the soul of a great person before our Lord. At a distance our Lord seems to be a harsh master bearing a crown of thorns upon his head and a cross upon his shoulders. We fear lest having him we must have naught else besides. Then one day we meet our Lord, perhaps in sorrow or in pain, and we pass five minutes with him, and our whole outlook on him completely changes. We see now that the crown of thorns is the prelude to the halo of light and the Cross the prelude to the empty tomb, and then we hear him say sweetly:

All which I took from thee, I did but take,
Not for thy harm
But that thou mightest seek it in My arm:
All which thy child's mistake
Fancies as lost. I have stored for thee at home;
Rise, clasp my hand, and come....
For whom will thou find to love
Ignoble thee, save Me, save only Me.
Francis Thompson, *The Hound of Heaven*

At this point begins the third stage of sainthood, namely, exchange. There is a wrong impression in the world to the effect that following our Lord means giving up the world, abandoning friends, surrendering wealth, and losing all that life holds dear. If we fear that in having him we must have naught else besides, we have not begun to understand Christ.

Such is not really the case. Sanctity is not a question of relinquishing or abandoning or giving up something for Christ; it is a question of exchange. Our Lord never said it was wrong to love the world. He said only that it was a loss, for "what shall a person give in exchange for his soul?" Exchange is founded on the fact that there are two classes of goods: first, things that we can get along without; second, things we cannot get along without. I can very well get along without a dime, but I cannot get along without the bread that it will buy, and so I exchange one for the other. So, too, in the spiritual world. I soon learn that there are many things I can get along without, and as I grow in acquaintance with Christ, I find that I can get along without sin, but I cannot get along without his peace of conscience, and so I exchange one for the other. Later on, as I get to know him better, I find that I can get along without an innocent pleasure, but I cannot get along without the pleasure of daily communion with him, and so I exchange one for the other. I find, by a still deeper acquaintance, that I can get along without the world's goods, but not without the wealth of Christ's grace, and so I exchange one for the other, and that is the vow of poverty. I find that I can get along very well without the pleasures of the flesh, but I cannot get along without the pleasures of Christ's spirit, and I exchange the one for the other, and that is the vow of chastity. I find that I can get along very well without my own will, but I cannot get along without his, and so I exchange the one for the other, and that is the vow of obedience.

Thus the saint goes on exchanging one thing for another. And thus it is that in making himself poor, he became rich, and in making himself a slave, he became free. The gravitation of the earth grows weaker, and the gravitation of the stars grows stronger, until finally, when there is nothing left to exchange, like Paul he cries out, "For me to die is gain," because by that last exchange his gain is Christ in everlasting life.

Sanctity, then, is not giving up the world. It is exchanging the world. It is a continuation of that sublime transaction of the Incarnation in which Christ said to humanity:

"You give Me your humanity, I will give you My Divinity.
You give Me your time, I will give you My eternity.

You give Me your bonds, I will give you My
    omnipotence.
You give me your slavery, I will give you My
    freedom.
You give Me your death, I will give you My life.
You give Me your nothingness, I will give you
    My all."

And the consoling thought throughout this whole transforming process is that it does not require much time; it
requires only much love.

Twenty-Three

Liberation

BEGINNING WITH THE abstract, there's a very close relation-ship between demonology and eschatalogy, between the devil and the world as it is and the world that is to be. Saint John tells us that the world is under the godless one. Remember this is not the original creation. We are living in a kind of second creation. We are living in the days of the Second Man, in the days of the New Israel. In the first chapter of Genesis we read God made the heavens and the earth; that there was a darkness and a void over the earth. In the book of Isaiah we read that God did not make the earth a void, and the same Hebrew word is used. Where did it come from? That's just like saying, for example, my mother made an angel food cake and it turned out to be a devil's food cake. Immediately we have creation and immediately we have chaos. Maybe it was due to the fall of the angels. In any case, thistles grew; beasts became wild; man had to eat his bread with the sweat of his brow. Earthquakes, floods, Ice Ages, natural catastrophes: This is not the original plan. Plan-ets, burned-out cinders, floating in the immensity of space. So something happened to this cosmos of ours. We know that God remade man, he made a new man—Christ—start-ing a new humanity. Why did he not make a new creation?

Sitting on a board of theology, I once asked this ques-tion: "Why, if all creation became disordered as a result of sin, why was there not pantheism instead of the Incarnation?" One of the other professors threw me off the board for asking such a question. But I thought it was rather simple that if the world became disordered through man it would begin to be ordered through man. Now let us see why Christ came to this earth. Here we are taking not a negative point of view but one given to us by Saint John himself. And he uses the word "very" to describe it. We read in 1 John, "The Son of God appeared for the very purpose of undoing the devil's work. *Undoing the devil's work*—in the cosmos, in man. Does not Saint Paul, in a beautiful passage in Philippians, say that Christ was born a slave. The word *douleuo*—slave, not servant—is used thirty-eight times in the New Testament. "Liberation" is used sixty-six times. So our Lord was born a slave. Putting it in more modern language, he was born in slavery. Yes, he was the Son of the heavenly Father. But was he not like, for example, one born in our own country more than a hundred years ago, subjected to slavery from the beginning? Was not our Lord shackled? When he became man, if he became our liberator, would he not have to break one bond after another? Were there not chains, as it were, about his hands and feet, so that as he began to take mastery over the world that was made for him and by him, he would snap one chain, then another, and then another, finally to liberate this great cosmos and, above all, to liberate us.

First, the cosmos. He walked on the waters, master of the waters. All the flood waters that became so errant and destructive now were submissive just to his feet. The winds and the seas—they, too, are not always rational to us, it seems. So he had to break that chain that the devil had over creation; and the apostles themselves were amazed. "Who is this that the winds and the seas obey him?" The fishes of the sea, too. "Peter, go out to the water." He goes to the water and finds the fish that has the bait in it. Then the animals. What kind of animal did he ride on Palm Sunday?

A colt—an ass—on which no man had ever ridden. A virgin for birth, a tomb in which no one had ever been buried, and an ass on which no one had ever been ridden. Just let any one of us try to take a young ass into a crowd of two million people who were gathered, amidst shrieking and waving of palms—so much so that it annoyed the Pharisees—and have complete mastery over this colt! Our Blessed Lord on that day became the patron saint of cowboys. He was making creation subject to him.

Whence come our diseases, whatever disease it happens to be? Well, the first cause is Satan. Maybe that is the reason there is so much in Scripture about the devil—like, for example, the woman who had been bound for so many years with her hemorrhage. It was not because people were very primitive in their belief. Scripture was simply stating first causes, not secondary causes. And the devil was the first cause. Just as our Lord mastered the cosmos, he now begins to break the chains of disease: He touches a leper, snaps another link, even allows a sacramental sign of the hem of his garment in order to cure an issue of blood. The blind, the deaf, those with palsied limbs—all these that were in some way related to the power of Satan over the world. Now he shows his control, so that at the end of his public life John could say that if he had written down all of the miracles that our Blessed Lord had worked, the world would not be large enough to contain the books thereof. So he has almost now liberated man. But there was what Saint Paul called "the last enemy." The last enemy was death. And our Blessed Lord gave to the earth the only serious wound it ever received: the wound of an empty tomb. He rose from the dead, the firstborn of the dead, and we've already risen with him. Thus, Christ came to this earth for the very purpose of undoing the work of Satan.

It was at the Cross—it's always the Cross—that Jesus threw off the powers of Satan. In Saint Paul's Letter to the

Colossians (2:14–15), we read: "[F]or he has canceled the bonds which pledged us to the decrees of the law. He stood it against us, but set it aside, nailing it to the Cross. And on the Cross he discarded the cosmic powers and authorities like a garment." The Greek word used means "reflexive." He threw them off. Threw off principalities and powers and made a public spectacle of them. But before he overcame these evil powers, how is it we could read, for example, in Job, "God said to Satan, 'Where have you been?' and Satan says, 'roaming around the earth.' 'Have you seen my servant Job?'" How does Satan get there?

Also, in Ezekiel, we have the angel of the Lord, who was a kind of theophany of Christ, defend Joshua the high priest, who takes off his filthy garments in the face of the accuser. How did this accuser get there? It must be that Scripture was taking heaven not as we do—as the place of the glorified—but as simply the entire cosmos, so that even the adversary, the Satan, had to be somewhere in God's dominion. How is he thrown out of heaven? Who could overcome him? He could be overcome, Scripture says, only by the power of the Cross. That was why, as our Blessed Lord got closer to Calvary, he became closer to the exiling of Satan from heaven. So our Blessed Lord said, "I saw Satan falling from heaven." And when our Blessed Lord completed redemption, liberated humanity, then there would be a complete exile of the satanic.

War broke out in heaven. Michael and his angels waged war upon the dragon. The dragon and his angels fought, but they had not the strength to win, and no foothold was left in heaven. So the great dragon was thrown down. That serpent of old that led the whole world astray, known as Satan, was the devil thrown down to the earth and his angels with him. "Then I heard a voice from heaven proclaiming aloud, 'This is the hour of the victory of our God, the hour of his sovereignty and power, when this Christ comes to his rightful rule, where the accuser of our brothers is over-thrown, who day and night accuse them before our God, by the sacrifice of the lamb they have conquered them.'" So the battle against Satan was won by the blood of Christ. For that is the only way that sins are ever forgiven.

Now, if Christ liberated us why did he not liberate the cosmos? In this late day of creation we're troubled by pollu-tion, and nature almost seems to turn against us. Will na-ture ever be completely liberated? Yes. Scripture tells us it is waiting for the liberation of the sons of God. When the num-ber of the elect is completed, then there will be a new heaven and a new earth. Saint Paul has a beautiful description of that in Romans:

> For created universe waits with eager expectation for God's sons to be revealed. It was made the vic-tim of frustration, not by its own choice. Nature did not become rebellious because it willed it, but be-cause of him who made it so. Because of us. Yet al-ways there was hope, because the universe itself is to be freed from the shackles of mortality and enter upon the liberty and splendor of the children of God. Up to the present, we know, the whole created uni-verse groans in all of its parts, as if in the pangs of childbirth (8:20–22).

Just think of it. We hardly think of nature that way. No poet has ever sung about nature being like a woman in child-birth, and yet here it is. We can hardly wait: each sunrise, each sunset. Nature is expectant. *When* will people serve God and the number of the elect be complete? Paul contin-ues:

> Not only so, but even we, to whom the Spirit has given its first fruits of the harvest to come, are groan-

ing inwardly where we wait for God to make us his sons and set our whole body free (8:23).

This, then, is liberation. It is not as the world understands it. Whenever the word "liberation" is used in Scripture, it is always as liberation from evil. It is not liberation from the commandments. It is not liberation from the Church. It is not liberation from family life. It is not liberation from morality. Liberation is from *evil*. See how the world has turned it around and made it a liberation from good. From morality and decency.

Our work is liberation. This refers to the individual order, to the social order, to the cosmos. Our interest must be as universal as the Christ whom we represent. How, then, do we really become true liberators? When do we begin to be effective in liberating souls from evil? Having power over nature? Within the answer lies the paradox of Christianity: by being slaves, slaves of Christ. That's what we are: the *douleuo*s of the good Lord.

The Romans had a custom called a triumphant procession. In order that anyone would have a triumphant procession—it happened only once every fifty years—there were several conditions that had to be observed: (1) Five thousand of the enemy had to be killed in a single engagement; (2) Vast territory had to be won for the Roman Empire; and (3) The general had to distinguish himself for bravery. If these conditions were fulfilled, then he would have a triumphant procession. The triumphant procession was led by the senate body. It also included the white bull that was to be sacrificed, followed by the captives and the spoils. You can imagine the triumphant procession, for example, after the conquest of Jerusalem. After the captives and the spoils came the priests with the incense, and then behind the priest was the emperor, dressed in purple, who wore the diadem of Jupiter; and amidst all manner of shouting he enters Rome.

Now Saint Paul must have seen that procession, because he describes it. He does not tell us which one. And what was interesting about it, and Saint Paul observed it closely, was that the incense which came from the thuribles of the priests had a sweet smell to all the Romans; but to the slaves it must have had a kind of hellish odor. Now we come to Saint Paul's description in which we are slaves of Christ: "Thanks be to God who continually leads us about, captives in his triumphal procession." That's what we are: captives—in Christ's triumphant procession. And everywhere he uses us to reveal and spread abroad the fragrance of the knowledge of himself. We are indeed the incense offered by Christ to God, both for those who are on their way to salvation, and those who are on their way to perdition. For the latter, it is a deadly fume that kills. To the former, a vital fragrance that brings life.

So…the secret is out: Christ has won the battle! And we are slaves in his triumphant procession.

Twenty-Four

"To Mother"

IT WAS MARY who gave to Jesus his human life—gave him hands with which to bless children; feet with which to go in search of stray sheep; eyes with which to weep over dead friends and a corrupt civilization; and a body with which he might suffer. It was through this Mother that he became the bridge between the divine and the human. If we take her away, then either God does not become man, or he that is born of her is a man, and not God. Without her we would no longer have our Lord.

If we have a box in which we keep our money, we know the one thing we must always give attention to is the key; we never think that the key is the money, but we know that without the key we cannot get into our money. The Mother of the babe is like that key; without her we cannot get to our Lord, because he came through her. She is not to be compared to our Lord, for she is a creature and he is the Creator. But without her we could not understand how the bridge was built between heaven and earth.

As she formed Jesus in her body, so she forms Jesus in our souls. In this one woman virginity and motherhood are united, as if God willed to show that both are necessary for the world. Those things which are separated in other creatures are united in her. The Mother is the protector of the Virgin, and the Virgin is the inspiration of Motherhood.

One cannot go to a statue of a mother holding a babe, hack away the mother, and expect to have the babe. Touch her and you spoil him. She is the window through which our humanity first catches a glimpse of divinity on earth. Perhaps she is more like a magnifying glass that intensifies our love of her Son and makes our prayers more bright and burning. He is the sun, she is the moon. On dark nights we are grateful for the moon; when we see it shining we know there must be a sun. So in this dark night of the world when people turn their backs on him who is the Light of the world, we look to Mary to guide our feet while we await the sunrise.

> With our forlorn and cheerless condition,
> Sweet Queen, we pray,
> give us patience and endurance.
>
> When our spirit is exalted or depressed,
> when it loses its balance,
> when it is restless or wayward,
> when it is sick of what it has
> and hankers after what it has not...
>
> When our mortal frame trembles
> under the shadow of the tempter,
> we shall call on Thee,
> and ask Thee to bring us back to ourselves,
> for Thou art the cool breath
> of the immaculate,
> the fragrance of the rose of Sharon—
>
> Thou art the Paradise of the Incarnation...
> Thou art Our Queen—
> Our Mother—
> Our Immaculate Mother,
> and we love Thee!

Twenty-Five

The Fullness of Christ

SAINT PAUL SPEAKS of Christ *emptying* himself, and also of the Church as being the "*fullness* of Christ." These words can be applied both to the historical life of our Lord—in the sense that Good Friday was the "emptying"—and Easter Sunday—its "filling up" in the glory of the Resurrection. I would like to correlate the Cross and the crown not in relation to those three days, but to the great cosmic plan, which embraces time and eternity, the Good Friday of creation and the Easter Sunday of heaven.

First of all, the history of God emptying himself. All goodness empties itself in the sense that it tends to diffuse and to communicate its goodness. The sun is good, and it empties itself in light and heat; the flowers are good, and they empty themselves in the riotous colors of their petals and the perfume of their silken chalices; animals are good, and they empty themselves in the generation of their young; man is good, and he empties himself in the communication of thoughts, and above all else by sacrifice, born and begotten of unselfish love. Now God is Perfect Goodness, for he possesses within himself the fullness of life, of truth, and of love in the amiable society of Father, Son, and Holy Spirit. Therefore, since he is goodness itself we expect him to diffuse and communicate his goodness.

That process by which Divine Love opened the fountains of the Godhead and poured them out is called by Saint

Paul the emptying of God—not an emptying in the sense that he lost what he gave, for he no more lost his perfection by giving than we lose anything by loving our friends, or by looking at our image in a mirror. Rather, he emptied himself in the sense that others began to share that which before was unshared.

Divine Love did not empty itself all at once. Only progressively through the ages did love pour itself out in ever increasing breaths until he had given all. He permitted creatures furtive glances behind the curtain of his divinity, for the complete vision if given all at once would have been too great for man, as a bright light sometimes blinds rather than illumines. The first outpouring of the chalice of Divine Love was at the beginning of time. Love could not contain the torrents of its power and goodness, and he emptied himself of them and told them to nothingness: That was Creation. Love could not keep the secrets of his heart, so he emptied himself of them and told them to mankind: That was Revelation. Love tends to become like the one loved. God loved humanity, and so he emptied himself and was found in the form and habit of humans: That was the Incarnation. Love also gives itself to the one loved, and if need be suffers and dies, for greater love than this no one has that he lay down his life for his friends: That was Redemption.

Love by its very nature tends to unity, not only in the flesh but in the spirit. Unity in the flesh was the Incarnation. The final emptying of Divine Love came when he poured out not his blood on the Cross, but his Spirit on the Church on the day of Pentecost. That was the birth of his Mystical Body.

There was nothing more that Divine Love could do. He had emptied himself of his power and wisdom in Creation, of his secrets in Revelation, of his majesty in the Incarnation, of his body and blood in the Redemption, and of his Spirit in the Church. Well indeed might love say, "What more can I do for my vineyard than I have done? From the chalice of my love I have poured forth even the last drop. I have kept back nothing. I have given you all that is mine as God." Truly indeed might Saint Paul say: *He emptied himself.*

Now let us look at the other side of the picture. All love is reciprocal: I love and I am loved. The love that spends itself is to be loved in return, for every emptying implies a filling. The emptying of the river calls for the filling of the ocean. The emptying of the valleys demands the fullness of the mountains. The emptying of the strength, youth, and lifeblood of parents is filled by the charms and radiance of their children. Everywhere the story is the same. The Cross cries out to the grave, the humiliation to the exaltation, and the Good Friday to the Easter Sunday. The reason is obvious: Love is not sterile, but a patient usurer who gets back his own in time. If, then, love is fecund and productive, if love by its very nature cries out for love in return, then surely the Divine Love that empties itself must be filled. The downward course of his love striking the mirror of our hearts must be reflected back again in heaven. Then, like the planets that travel in orbits, the Divine Love that was sent out to the circle of this universe would once more return to its starting point filled with the myriad loves of creatures it met on the way.

If God has emptied himself of Divine Love, then he should be filled with it in the hearts of men; if he has poured forth, then he should be replenished; if he has drained his chalice, then it should be filled again. And at this point begins the history of the filling; or the story of how man loved God because God first loved man. If the story of the "emptying" of God stretches in history from Creation to the descent of the Holy Spirit, then the story of the filling reaches from the descent to the final glorification of the Kingdom of Heaven, or the return of the Prodigal Love back again to the

Father's house. In a word, the growth of the Mystical Body of Christ is the story of the "filling up" of Christ to his full stature in the glory of the celestial Jerusalem.

And these are the stages of the "filling." The love of God that emptied itself in Creation is filled as the Church lays hold of material things, breathes over them the words "Praise the Lord," and thus makes them pay tribute to the Creator. The gold in the bowels of the earth, the wheat in the field, the grapes in the vineyard, the trees of the forest, cannot of themselves thank God; but the Church, by putting gold in the chalice, wheat and grapes in her Mass, wood in the crucifixes, thus "fills up" unto God the very love that he once poured out in creating them.

The love of God that emptied itself of his secrets in Revelation is filled up by the faith of the Church in the [hundreds of millions of] Catholics throughout the world who chant her Credo and profess unto death that they believe every truth Christ teaches "because he can neither deceive nor be deceived."

The Love that emptied itself in the Incarnation by God becoming man is now filled and returned by the Church, by incorporating to that Spirit millions and millions of souls who for twenty centuries have lived the life of the one Body, have been vivified by the same Spirit, and have been obedient to the one Head.

If you would know the extent of the growth of the fullness of Christ in his Mystical Body, then think of how much a human organism grows from the moment of conception. In the course of its life millions and millions of cells have been unified and vivified by the soul that came into the original cell at the moment of its origin. But even that is an inadequate human analogy for what Saint Paul calls the fullness of Christ, which is the Church. There is no way of adequately measuring the amount of faith, hope, and love that has been returned by the Church to God since the day of Pentecost.

But since the Church is a living personality, because it has the same soul, the same head, the same mind, the same heart, the same life now as it had [two thousand] years ago, she can tell us of her growth and fullness in the first person.

And these are the words of the Church on the fullness of Christ:

On the day of Pentecost there were twelve cells in my body besides the Blessed Mother who was left to be my mother and nurse during infancy. My body first began to grow within the nursery of Judaism where I had my birth; but within a few short years I had incorporated unto myself even the Gentiles who knew no God but Caesar. My Spouse, Christ, had told me that I would be hated as he was hated, and while still an infant there were other Herods who would have slain me in Rome, as they would have slain him in Bethlehem. I have had but few moments of peace. From the outside I was attacked by the sword; from the inside I was abused by false brethren. And yet neither persecution nor error has stopped my growth. The sword strengthened my courage, and error sharpened my intellect.

In a century I had grown until I filled the Roman Empire, and then beyond its outposts I sent forth missionaries to the barbarians who helped me grow unto that fullness I had when I crowned Charlemagne in the year 800. My body grew in age and grace and strength and in the twelfth century of my existence, like Christ in the twelfth year, I was instructing the doctors of the world in the temples of the medieval universities. In the sixteenth century I lost some cells of my body, as I had lost some before in the errors of the Gnostics and Pelagians. And yet after each loss there came new strength, for my lot, like that of my

Spouse Christ, is to be ever rising from the tomb where men can leave me as dead. And so I chastened myself at the Council of Trent and brought myself into subjection, and now at this very hour the twelve cells whom I numbered in my body on Pentecost have grown to [several hundred million] souls in every corner of the globe.

But in the course of my life [of 2000 years], like the life of a human body, some of my cells have died and been replaced by others—but I have remained the same, because my soul is the abiding Spirit of God. Some of my members have been gathered into the Church Triumphant, where they enjoy blessedness with my Spouse Christ; others of my members who, while they were with me in the Church Militant, sinned and atoned not, are now gathered in purgatory, which is the Church Suffering where they wash their baptismal robes clear for the Spotless King in the glory of heaven.

How much longer I shall live on this earth, how much time awaits the consummation, I know not. But when the number of the elect is completed, when the seats vacated by the fallen angels are filled, when I shall have grown to my full stature, then shall the end come; then shall the Church Militant on earth and the Church Suffering in purgatory be gathered into the unity of the Church Triumphant in heaven, on the glorious Easter that shall never end because there is no time with God but only eternal love.

And would you know the fullness of Christ; would you know the final end of the Mystical Body of Christ; would you know what will happen on that Easter Day when Christ the Head and I his Body are united in heaven? Then listen to my words as I set them down through John in the Apocalypse:

I saw a new heaven and a new earth. And I saw
the holy city, the new Jerusalem coming down out
of heaven from God prepared as a bride adorned
for her husband. And I heard a great voice from the
throne saying, "Behold the tabernacle of God with
men, and he will dwell with them. And they shall be
his people; and God himself with them shall be their
God. And God shall wipe away all tears from their
eyes; and death shall be no more, nor mourning,
nor crying, nor sorrow shall be any more, for the
former things are passed away." ...And he showed
me the holy city of Jerusalem coming down out of
heaven from God, having the glory of God, and the
light thereof was like to a precious stone as to the
jasper stone, even as crystal. And it had a wall great
and high, having twelve gates, and in the gates twelve
angels, and names written thereon, which are the
names of the twelve tribes of the children of Israel.
On the east, three gates; and on the north, three
gates; and on the south, three gates; and on the west,
three gates. And the wall of the city had twelve foundations, and in them, the twelve names of the twelve
apostles of the Lamb.... And the building of the wall
thereof was of jasper stone: but the city itself pure
gold, like to clear glass. And the foundations of the
walls of the city were adorned with all manner of
precious stones.... And the twelve gates are twelve
pearls, one to each...and the street of the city was
pure gold, as it were transparent glass. And I saw
no temple therein. For the Lord Almighty is the
temple thereof and the Lamb. And the city hath no
need of the sun, nor of the moon, to shine in it. For
the glory of God hath enlightened it, and the Lamb
is the lamp thereof....

And I saw a great multitude which no man could

number of all nations, and tribes, and peoples, and tongues, standing before the throne, and in sight of the Lamb.... And all the angels stood round about the throne, and the ancients, and the four living creatures: and they fell down upon their faces, and adored God, saying, "Amen. Benediction and glory, and wisdom, and thanksgiving, honor and power and strength to our God for ever and ever. Amen."

Revelation 21:1–23; 7:9; 7:11–12

Such is the end and destiny of the Church, which Saint Paul describes as the fullness of Christ. It was born of the emptying of God's love; it is filled by all the virgins and martyrs, confessors and pontiffs, saintly mothers and fathers, devoted husbands and wives, sacrificing missionaries and apostolic priests, simple children who never grew wise with the false wisdom of the world, and all members of Christ's Mystical Body who once again filled up the Divine Chalice with love, which Love drained in making and redeeming us.

Thus the end of the chapter of time will be when the Mystical Body of Christ, which is his Church, will have grown to its fullness, just as the glory of the physical body of Christ came when it had reached its fullness on Good Friday and Easter Sunday. The end of history will come at the moment when Love which came down from heaven in an Emmanuel disguised in lowliness, becomes transfigured in its fullness as the Church, the glory of the Great Original, the Lamb of God who takes away the sins of the world. Evil will end when the last baptized child, hewn from the great quarry of humanity, shall be shaped and squared and cut for service in the great living temple whose architect is Love— which is God.

Twenty-Six

Ignorant of the World

Oh Jesus, I do not want to know the world.
I do not want to know the pride of the world
which crowns Thy head with thorns.
I do not want to know how nails of selfishness
    are driven,
nor how the spear of bitterness is launched.

I do not want to know
how snowflakes are hammered,
nor who turns about the Arcturus.
I do not want to know the length
of this great universe
and its expanse in light-years.

I do not want to know the breadth of the earth
as it dances about the chariot of the sun.
I do not want to know the heights of the stars
as they glitter about the day's dead sanctities.
I do not want to know the depth of the sea
nor the secrets of its palace.

I am willing to be ignorant of all these things.
I want only to know one thing,
and that is—the breadth and length
and depth and height

of Thy redeeming love on the Cross,
Sweet Savior of all.

I want, dear Jesus,
to be ignorant of everything
in this world—everything—
but You!
And then, by the strangest
of strange paradoxes,
I shall be wise!

Twenty-Seven

The Church Speaks

To his accusers' questions, our Lord gave only the answer of his withering silence. From a worldly point of view, he did the foolish thing. What would you think of someone before a court who might clear himself of a charge by a word, or a show of power, and yet refuses to do so? Well, here is our Lord going to the Cross and to death, simply because he will not do the worldly thing. That was foolishness. The folly of Omnipotence!

And from that day to this, the Church has been robed in the garment of a fool, because she never does the worldly thing. Her saints are fools, because they plunge after poverty like others dig after gold, tear at their body while others pamper theirs, and dare even to swing the world a trinket at their wrist, in order that they might gain an everlasting crown. Her devout nuns are fools who leave the lights and glamours of the world for the shades and shadows of the Cross, where saints are made; her priests are fools because they practice celibacy in a world that has gone crazy about sex. The Vicar, the Pontiff, is a fool, for refusing to relax the teachings of Christ. Yes, the Church is a fool, and all her loyal members are fools, but they are fools only from the world's point of view, not from God's point of view. For with the foolish things of the world God has chosen to confound the wise, and with the weak things of the world to confound the strong.

The Church must always bear the taunt of being unmodern and unworldly, as our Lord had to bear it before Herod. And our Lord warned us that it would be the mark of the divinity of the Church: "If you had been of the world, the world would love its own; but because you are not of the world, but I have chosen you out of the world, therefore the world hates you.... If the world hates you, know that it has hated me before you." In other words: "If you ever want to discover my religion on the face of the earth, look for the Church that does not get along with the world." The religion that gets on with the world, and is accepted by it, is worldly; the religion that does not get on with the world is other-worldly, which is another way of saying that it is divine.

The Church is very modern, if modern means serving the times in which we live, but she is not modern, if modern means believing that whatever is modern is necessarily true. The Church is modern, if modern means that her members should change their hats with the seasons, and even with the styles, but she is not modern if it means that every time someone changes his hat, he should also change his head, or in an applied sense, that she should change her idea of God every time psychology puts on a new shirt, or physics a new coat.

The Church is modern, if modern means incorporating the newfound wisdom of the present with the heritage of the centuries, but she is not modern if it means sneering at the past as one might sneer at someone's age. She is modern, if modern means a passionate desire to know the truth, but she is not modern if it means that truth changes with the calendar, and that what is true on Tuesday is false on Wednesday. The Church is modern, if modern means progress toward a fixed ideal, but she is not modern if it means changing the ideal instead of attaining it.

The Church is like an old schoolmaster—the schoolmaster of the centuries—and as such she has seen so many students pass before her, cultivate the same poses, and fall into the same errors, that she merely smiles at those who believe that they have discovered a new truth; for in her superior wisdom and experience, she knows that many a so-called new truth is only a new label for an old error.

It is about time that the modern world gave up expecting the Church to die because she is "behind the times." Really she is behind the scenes, and knows just when the curtain will fall on each new fad and fancy. If an announcement had been made a thousand times about a death, and the funeral never took place, people would soon begin to take the announced funeral as a joke. And so it is with the Church. She is always supposed to be behind the times, and yet it is she who lives *beyond* the times.

At least a hundred voices in every century since her birth have tolled the bells for her funeral, but the corpse never appeared. They are always buying coffins for her, but it is they who use the coffins. They are always assisting at her apparently last breath, and yet she moves. They are always digging her grave, and it is a grave into which the diggers fall. The taunt that she is "behind the times" and "out of touch with the world" will never annoy her, for she knows that it is easy to be in the swim, in the sense of being "up to the times," for even a dead body can float downstream.

It takes a live Body to resist the current.

Twenty-Eight

The Resurrection Continues

THE RESURRECTION of Christ, like the Incarnation and Passion, is a continuing process. Nothing new is in the world. Only the same old things are happening to new people, as is proven by the "news on the hour." What plane will be skyjacked tomorrow? Who will be murdered? Hidden in the media's love of the tragic is not only a hidden death wish, but also an unconscious concern with the ultimate: death. Accidents, muggings, assassinations are interesting as penultimates because they avoid facing the ultimate. The same is true of the passion for revolution and the despisal of the past. One would almost think to hear revolutionaries speak that they were born without navels—having no debt or bond or cord to the past. For the first time they no longer think about history, so as to avoid old errors with new labels; rather, they seek consciously to create history as a "now."

But this forgets that what Easter did was to create the "new." The Church became the "new" Israel, and each person a "new creature." "When anyone is united to Christ, there is a new world. The old order has gone, and a new order has already begun" (2 Cor 5:17).

The Resurrection, if regarded so exclusively as *past*, finds its vision is limited to the empty tomb; if directed exclusively to the *future*, it zeroes in on judgment and the final resurrection. But if the Resurrection is progressive, and based on Christ's victory over death, then it affects me *now*. The Resurrection is not just hope in the sense of futurity, as Ernest Bloch would have us believe. Oscar Wilde's remark is here apropos: that a world map which fails to display the land of Utopia hardly deserves a glance. Nor is credence to be put in Bultmann's view, which ignores the historical part of the Resurrection and makes it only mythological or subjective. According to this view what matters is the "now," not whether Christ really rose from the dead. Nor may one so eliminate the future and the transcendent as does Feuerbach, who would "transform theologians into anthropologists, lovers of God into lovers of man, candidates for the next world into students of this world, religious and earthly monarchs and lords into free, self-reliant citizens of earth."

Nowhere in Scripture does belief in the Resurrection as a fact and as a hope militate against responsibility to earth, but rather "brings healing for all mankind" and demands "living a life of temperance, honesty and godliness in the present age" (Titus 2:12). The Christian is one who simultaneously rejoices in hope and endures affliction: "Let hope keep you joyful; in trouble stand firm; persist in prayer."

The Resurrection is not just something that happened; it is something still happening. And it continues because it happened once, like a great cosmic explosion that sent the planets spinning and in constant motion.

The perfect person goes to a triple crucifixion in order to attain a corresponding triple resurrection:

1. Death to the womb and birth to human life.
2. Death to human nature and birth to participation in the Divine nature.
3. Death to death and birth to the Glorious Resurrection.

If we were conscious in the darkness of the womb, would

we not have shrunk to have left its security for an unknown life? If some agnostic could have addressed us he might have said: "Do you really believe there is another life than prenatal life? What evidence have you who live in darkness that there is such a thing as light? Why barter away the security of nourishment without effort for the insecurity of 'pie in the sky'? You may have faith that there is another world than the one you experience, but your faith is subjective and so void of any scientific certitude of another life."

But would we not have answered that person: "Listen! See these arms of mine laid across my breast, with fingers at their tips? Would I have ever formed them, unless I could touch something and hold somebody like myself? My eyes have a capacity for seeing, my ears for hearing, though I never saw a sun or heard a symphony. My legs! Useless they are now, but were they not made for playing, for walking, for running? I am made for another world, even though my senses have never seen it. Some day the particle of flesh that entombs me will burst with a momentary cry of Calvary's agony of birth, and then will come the joy of light and music and friendship."

Humanity is made up of two kinds of people: the "once-born" and the "twice-born"—the once-born who left a tomb of flesh with a cry, and the twice-born who are "born of God" and made partakers not only of the nature of their parents, but of the nature of God. Physical birth is the coming into a natural environment.

But a person cannot be coerced into spiritual relationship; it demands consent and must be self-determined. This second birth is more flesh-shattering and catastrophic than the first, and more umbilical cords are broken than in seeing the light of day. If a block of marble bloomed, that would be something beyond its nature and capacity, and if the man of flesh becomes a spiritual man, this is the kind of birth that demands not only the services of the Divine Obstetrician, but also the will to "die" on the part of the fetus. First is the dying to self in union with the Cross, then the Easter of an inner peace nothing can shatter.

But before I can attain that birth, I must hear: "If anyone wishes to be a follower of mine, he must leave self behind; he must take up his cross and come with me" (Mt 16:24). But the Cross is no self-mutilation or masochism. It is a plucking off of dead buds so that the new buds may blossom; it is the pruning of a tree for a richer harvest; it is the dull rehearsal for the triumph of a concert. *God is not the God of dead things, but of renewed things. He does not change the ideal to fit the way people live; but he changes the way people live to give them the ideal.* Only the person who elects to live for himself remains in the tomb. No self-denial is ever without a resurrection of the spirit; in each newborn soul there is verified: "Now at the place where he had been crucified, there was a garden" (Jn 19:41).

The last womb through which we pass is the womb of time to give birth to eternity. Death is the last penalty for sin; it is the Golgotha that individualizes us, regardless of how conformist we were in life. Here we step out of the ranks as our name is called; a line is drawn beneath the sum of days, and that is the computer slip we carry to judgment. During life many of our decisions were imperfect because flesh, time, and a momentary advantage confused the issue. But when the bird is released from the cage, it flies; so at death the wings of the spirit of man in the light of his previous graces makes the ultimate and final decision of being for or against Christ.

"I believe in the resurrection of the body" is the Easter that the person looks forward to after his last breath on the Cross of life. In 1 Corinthians 15:35–50 Saint Paul resorts to the Lord's analogy of the seed. The seed that is planted in the ground does not rise with the same body that was buried. The new one is quite different, though definitely related to it. The Easter of the divinized person is not just the reward of an immortal soul. The Resurrection is not soul-salvation, but person-salvation. Since Christ the Head of a regenerated Body rose, then the members are ontologically bound up with his Resurrection: "But the truth is, Christ was raised to life—the first fruits of the harvest of the dead" (1 Cor 15:20). The ancient Jewish law obliged the farmer to bring the first fruit of the harvest and "wave it before the Lord" as a token that the whole field and the farmer himself belonged to God. Christ is that "first fruit" of our humanity. With all our failings, we are dedicated to him in our prayers, our works, our sicknesses, and our joys. Our resurrection is assured, though it does require the last configuration, Christ, sharing in his death to share in his glory. As we might have shrunk from breaking the umbilical cord, so we shrink from shattering the cords of time. Christ came not to negate life, but to give it more abundantly. Anyone who ever denied himself a theft or an adultery has already placed death in the middle of his or her life as the condition of peace of conscience. All such acts stem not from our instinct of life, but from our wisdom of death. *Christ leads me through no darker rooms than he has gone before.*

When a person is raised up from his own dead past to a goodness which in terms of the past cannot be accounted for, he is face to face with the miracle of the Creed: "I believe in the Resurrection." Or when a person is able to take the worst the world can give, and make it contribute to his spiritual growth, he has modernized the miracle of the seed "which is the Word." As Dietrich Bonhoeffer wrote from his prison, "Who am I? They mock me, these lovely questions of mind. Whoever I am, Thou knowest, O God, I am Thine." The only ones who suffer from the problem of identity are those who have no goal, no destiny, no eternal shore. How do we know the identity of New York State? By its boundaries. How do we know the identity of a baseball diamond? By its foul lines. How do we know our identity? By limits, by laws, by destinies, by God. Once the Good Friday/ Easter Sunday syndrome is made the rule of life, then one sees that only the Christ-fettered are free.

I am not my own; I am his. What person anyway has not had in his own personal life a thousand falls, a thousand resurrections? Into what open graves has he walked, and ere the dust was piled the winding sheets of the old self were left behind? Every time one's knee bends in confession, he admits to the crucifixion of his Lord, and when his wiggling feet, like worms, stick out from under the veil, he rises from the dead.

Epilogue

SHALL WE EXPECT *another* Christ? That is the question asked in the midst of disappointments and loneliness. No person at all times lives up to his or her highest level. Saints often fail in that very grace which was their most striking characteristic. Elijah, for example, failed in his courage, when he ran from Jezebel; Moses in his meekness, when he smashed the tablets of the Law; Peter in his intense love, when he denied; John had heard in prison the works of Christ, but he also heard how he ate with publicans and sinners. Likewise, priests, frustrated in what they believed to be their mission to identify Christ and politics or Christ and sociology, ask for "another Christ." The same is true of his Mystical Body: "Are you the Church founded on the Rock, or shall we look for another?" Shall we accept what has endured, or shall we look for "another"—a charismatic church?

At the very moment the messengers came, Jesus was healing "many sufferers from diseases, plagues, and evil spirits; and on many blind people he bestowed sight" (Lk 7:21). Saint Cyril reflects, "He knew as God what John's design was, and he put it into his heart to send the messengers when he was working miracles, the true answer to his questions." Then our Lord gave the deputation this answer:

> Go and tell John what you have seen and heard: how the blind recover their sight, the lame walk, the lep-

ers are made clean, the deaf hear, the dead are raised to life, the poor are hearing the good news. And happy is the man who does not find me a stumbling block (Lk 7:22–23).

It was evident that John was thinking the Kingdom of God "comes with observation," instead of through a slow, quiet stage of leaf and bud and full-grown fruit. To paraphrase Jesus' answer:

John, it is because I do not follow your method that I am He. Your method was drastic, uncompromising, and judicial. You are expecting me to act now the way I will act at the end of time, when axes and shovels and fire will cut down underbrush like Herods and winnow chaff like Herodias. You want me to call everything white or black, to be an economic reformer who will abolish slums and burn slumlords. You want me to blast Pentagons and Roman armies, to make a world where there are no more multiple sclerosis, migraine headaches, cancer. But this is not my mission.

When I come into the threshing floor I see not only wheat but human chaff that can be salvaged. Bring to me Magdalenes off the streets, and I will make them think of my Passion rather than their passions; lead to me those who believed God is dead, and I will show them how dead they were by bringing them to life; let those white with leprosy of sin but touch me, and they shall dine with me clean at the banquet of life, like Lazarus. I shall not break prison bars, but shall teach prisoners to be resigned to my will, for I, too, shall be in prison. I shall not shorten the life of "old fogies"—people who bore everyone—but I shall teach them how I have been bored with them, yet love them just the same.

The faith I require is not when there is money in the bank, but when there is bankruptcy; not to believe when the sun is shining, but when it is hidden. The seeming heedlessness of my divine power is never loveless, never an unwise delay. The evidence that I am He is not so much in what meets the eye, but when people in their hearts feel the need of me.

Happy the one who does not find me a stumbling block.

About the Author

ARCHBISHOP FULTON J. SHEEN (1895–1979) was one of the best known and best loved Catholic prelates of all time. Distinguished philosopher, orator, preacher, teacher, missionary, radio and television personality, and author, he held a J.C.B. degree from Catholic University, a Ph.D. from the University of Louvain, an S.T.D. from the Angelicum in Rome, and numerous honorary degrees. His oral and written legacy is not only substantial, but enduring.

This volume is being published not only as a tribute on the occasion of the twentieth anniversary of Sheen's death, but in response to renewed strong interest in his work. Other titles available from Liguori are: *Peace of Soul; Lift Up Your Heart; Jesus, Son of Mary; Characters of the Passion; From the Angel's Blackboard;* and *Simple Truths.*

Sheen was born to eternal life on December 9, 1979, one day after the feast of the Immaculate Conception.